AF326801

The

Hathaway Equation

***The Plan to Halt
and Reverse Ecological Collapse***

by

Phillip Hathaway

Hardcastle Publishing
New York

to

Nidhi

Table of Contents

Author's Foreword

THE rumble of the bulldozer, its unfeeling roar as it mows down the old growth forest, comes across the river to my home with its soul-crushing sound. Over one thousand acres of virgin woodlands have been destroyed within three miles of my front door, their beauty raped, murdered. My friends who lived within them— the playful armadillos, coyotes, rabbits, and otters who lived along the riverbank, the many species of songbirds—have been killed or fled their ancestral homes of past centuries.

That clanking of the bulldozer's iron treads pricks my heart, reminding me of the darkest day of all my life— that mournful day I lost my dog, Blackjack, my dearest friend and guru of the higher virtues. Like the flora and fauna being crushed by the bulldozer, he was a divine ambassador sending a message of love, of hope. For they exude the same life-giving light that shone from within his blameless soul. And so, I dedicate, I consecrate this equation to them all. For I know quite confidently that, under its guidance, we can redeem the Earth from our species.

Yet, it seems most people say, "There's nothing we can do about it." Isn't this an insult to the one who most graciously gave us the Earth with its vast bounty, its multicolored elegance? However, for a moment, we will try to consider their perspective. Is it genuinely possible to do anything about the human destruction of life on Earth?

Is it possible to drink sparkling clean water and breathe pristine forest air within our largest cities? Could vast superhighways, streets, roads, and millions of acres of parking lots be replaced by immaculate fields, meadows, rivers, and streams while at the same time *improving* transportation? Can the wildlife we have lost in the last fifty years thrive as once before? Is it realistic to think that war, the accomplice of ecological recklessness, is not inevitable?

Under the auspices of the proposed equation, each question can be answered affirmatively. Of course, many people will doubt these words. Yet, should not the savant test them? Should not the peacemaker give them tepid consideration? For I do not claim to have every solution, merely the irreducible formula that shall lead to a self-perpetuating series of them, materializing within a new world.

And a new world we need. Three billion wild birds have been lost in the U.S. and Canada since 1970.[1] Plastic and debris float over an area three times the size of France in the Pacific Ocean.[2] Eighty thousand acres of forests disappear from the Earth each day.[3] Wildlife populations have declined by more than fifty percent on average in the last two generations.[4]

Therefore, it is not surprising that this rolling mega-death is causing extinction rates to be much higher than the organic norm.[5]

Its locomotive force is spurred ever faster with the burgeoning world population that will geometricize to

---

[1] *Decline of the North American avifauna,* (Washington, DC: American Association for the Advancement of Science, 2019)

[2] Lebreton, L., Slat, B., Ferrari, F. et al. *Evidence that the Great Pacific Garbage Patch is rapidly accumulating plastic.* (New York: Scientific Reports, 2018)

[3] "Measuring the Daily Destruction of the World's Rainforests," (New York: Scientific American, 2009)

[4] Elizabeth Ann Brown, "Widely misrepresented report still shows catastrophic animal decline," (Washington, DC: National Geographic, 2018).

[5] Nadia Drake, "Will Humans Survive the Sixth Great Extinction?" (Washington, DC: National Geographic, 2015)

approximately 11 billion souls by the year 2100, [6] [7] a threshold that, once crossed, may be irreversible. The high estimate, however, is 16 billion people by 2100.[8]

Indeed, the foreboding statistics of this looming ecological collapse are accelerating with such speed that they become outmoded before their printing. This, albeit, is not a book of data. Ample books and articles contain them, and these are quite essential to measure and eventually realize our overarching mission.

By contrast, I have only crafted a little compass that points to humankind's true north, that Polaris, which shall lead us away from our lostness, back to our safe home once again, and from there, to heights unimagined. To arrive there, we must begin at the only material beginning—our bodies. For unless we care for this inner ecosystem, it is unlikely that we shall properly care for the outer ecosystem. Indeed, the heroes and heroines of the flora and fauna live healthy lifestyles, and from this physical starting place, extend those nurturing habits to

---

[6] *World Population Prospects 2019*, (New York: The United Nations Department of Economic and Social Affairs, Population Division, 2019)

[7] Hoornweg, Daniel; Pope, Kevin, "Population predictions of the 101 largest cities in the 21st century," (Toronto: Global Cities Institute, 2014)

[8] Pison, Giles, "How many humans tomorrow? The United Nations revises its projections" (Melbourne: The Conversation, 2019)

out them. That is why I have consid-
nent such a healthy lifestyle. For, it can scarcely be overstated that without being good stewards of ourselves, it is improbable that we shall assume faithful stewardship of the blue and green miracles all around us. Like a pebble cast into a pond that makes ever-widening ripples of concentric circles, these life-giving ideas manifest in the world around good stewards of their bodies: cities designed for humans, lush vegetation, and even wildlife, rather than automobiles and the vast, deathly pallor of asphalt and concrete they require.

From there, population management will be a natural evolution implemented by benevolently appealing to the always-present desire to ease the weight of the human predicament while simultaneously offering a previously unseen path to a new world. A new path. A path at once higher and more luxurious, from which this present society will seem quite crude and pitifully backward.

Upon this mind expansion and the equation's proven practicality, enough members of society will experience a tangible life improvement to establish it as the norm. Once we are the beneficiaries of such advancements, once the social ladder has been elevated to such heights and at the same time broadened so that all may ascend, we may be reluctant to abandon it. This giant step forward shall be initiated and accomplished neither by law nor enforcement but rather by influencing public opinion, an integral subset of the equation. Of course, managing a population barreling toward 11 billion people may seem entirely new and different. Yet suppose that it was *noncompulsory* and had *nothing whatsoever to do with eugenics.* Imagine if such a plan was universally benevolent while conspicuously improving the lives of the world's weakest, poorest people.

Without such a collective, social innovation, could our alternative be global, cataclysmic extinction? So, let us not indulge those who behave as pouty and tantrum-prone toddlers, exploding in a shower of tears when encountering a new lesson. Let us lead the world as clear-minded adults, unafraid of "thoughtwork," as I call it. For humans have not implemented a successful plan to stop this steamroller of mindless morbidity that bears down upon us. Perhaps, at this last minute upon the biological clock, we should consider one. But only one that is a deviation from the norm will work since the norm is itself the very thing that has caused this extinction rate that is far above the organic benchmark. Indeed, the plan must be super-societal, as we know society—a new epoch unfolding and arising *posthaste* above the old, decaying one.

For example, I recall watching a football game in which one team was thirty-two points behind their opponents with only twenty-eight minutes left to play. The losing team, however, did not continue with their game plan but replaced it with a radically new one, and, miraculously, they won. Had they continued executing the same plays, they would have lost. This game represents a universal fact in all sports, business, and war: one must radically change one's game plan when losing. Likewise, we must embrace a decidedly different approach to our lives and all of life about us should we hope to halt and reverse ecological collapse.

Now, with population management comes the recession of encroachment upon wildlife habitat, which is the singular objective of many environmentalists alarmed by sprawling human demographics. Yet, there remains the divine summons to also redeem the *civilized* genre of the fauna. That shall be no easy task. It is a spiritual battle.

And a host of angels in dazzling white,
Fought the Battle of Earth against mankind,
Yet a remnant saw them a war waging,
In flashes of light against the darkness,
Breaking heaven's lance and sword for the Earth,
And allying with them, joined the battle,
Valiantly fighting to save all Earthly life.

And so, "The Battle of Earth" is my symbolic portrayal of our struggle. As to whether angels exist, I do not know. Yet as I fancifully depict them battling mankind in verse, it is more precise to say they are warring against wrongheaded ideas that humanity has cherished to its peril. "For we wrestle not against flesh and blood" in this ideological contest, in which we influence others by example.

That brings us to an integral point of our success: beyond opposing antiquated social norms, we must point to a new societal model that renders the present one obsolete. That, dear friends, must be the emphasis of our work. We wage a positive battle, therefore, by uplifting rather than condemning, by presenting the solution rather than mocking the mistake. For ours is a calling most noble.

Yet, when seeing the battle challenge described on the following pages and Grendel dominating the battlefield, who deviates so grotesquely from natural shape and size, some may feel a frightful weakness that gives way to retreat. Stand firm. We can subdue the monster, turning it into an opportunity for all humankind, indeed for all life upon Earth. But mark my words. Mark them and remember, as the Duke of Wellington said at the Battle of Waterloo, that it will be *the nearest run thing you ever saw in your life.*

To proceed most valiantly, we must know precisely, even intimately, what we seek to defend, fore to aft. And, as we arrive at omega by beginning at alpha, so we proceed to the complex by understanding the simple—the epiphany of the flora and fauna.

P. H.

July 29, 2018

The

Hathaway Equation

Chapter One

The Flora and Fauna

BEFORE we can become good stewards of the flora and fauna, or assume stewardship of them at all, we must know what or, more precisely, *who* they are. For we can never effectively assume the care and protection of things of such inestimable value, indeed, elements on which our next breath, our next sip of water, and our next morsel are utterly dependent, without truly understanding their nature. Therefore, before considering what their stewardship entails, let us seek to understand them by realizing that all the flora and fauna are representatives to the temporal world of something far more significant. We hope to be attuned to their eternal hymn. Yet at the same time, we are natural pragmatists who, for instance, do not yearn to pet poisonous snakes nor allow them in or near our homes. We simply know that the flora and fauna are telling us something—something important.

For clarity, it may be helpful to give thought to Plato's allegory of the cave, from which I take some creative liberties, deviating slightly from his original illustration.

Here, we find people sitting in a cave, facing the cave's wall with their backs to its opening. Being prisoners, they are chained without the ability to turn and face the cave's portal to the outside world of light with its breathtaking palette of colors and variegated life. Yet, sunlight shines into the cave, casting shadows upon the wall they face, and these, they believe, are all there is to the outside world. And so, in their life of bondage within the cave, they see only shadows—monotone gray shadows that can neither be grasped nor touched, void of aroma and taste. They are nothing more than one-dimensional apparitions, some of which briefly wisp about on the wall and just as quickly disappear.

One day, their chains are unshackled. They walk from the cave into the full world to fall upon their knees in weeping praise, beholding those who, unbeknownst to them, cast the familiar yet mundane shadows. One such shadow was cast by a stallion prancing playfully in defiance of gravity, his muscularity rippling with each step, his splendid blonde coat shimmering in the Sun's light.

Majestically, he flicks his white mane and tail then races across the open field before him with a grace that somehow proves the divine. Another shadow they learn was that of a jaguar, orange and dappled with a geometric pattern of black and yellow and white in striking contrast to his fire-green eyes that cautiously search the woebegone castaways. With fluidity and aplomb that bespeak deeper agility and strength, he nonchalantly walks past them.

The shadow of what the prisoners assumed was merely a tall bush that appeared upon the cave's wall, they discover with awe, is an oleander tree arrayed in her new blossoms, each saturated in deepest pink. Just beyond her is a meadow of verdant green where a thousand daffodils sway in full bloom, their yellow petals offering a cheery welcome to the real world, to these who were once lost but now are found. Beyond the daffodils is a vast forest of tall pines, reaching fifty feet and higher, stretching across the valley and onward, covering the surrounding hills. The shadows cast by a few of their treetops belied their myriad numbers, their true and emerald stateliness.

Another shadow was of a fair young lady. How could they have dreamt of the pastels of her face, her topaz eyes, her pink lips, her flaxen hair, her peach and golden complexion? How could they have imagined the kindness of her expression? With a carefree smile, she offers them a silver bowl, which she holds out to them with extended arms so shapely, soft, and slender. Within the bowl are succulent strawberries, oranges, apples, and purple grapes, their tastes and aromas causing an expatiation of the previously imprisoned senses of these reborn souls.

So are the flora and fauna of Earth shadows of a world more real than this, foretastes of the true world to come, ambassadors of the most high, each of whom must be revered as his messenger to us individually. Perhaps, we will be held accountable for our response to them as they have come into our lives. Yet let us be clear, dear friends, we shall receive fewer and fewer messages from the divine since there remain fewer and fewer messengers to send them.

For the sparkling lights of many colors all around us are passing away, and another world must grow old, then die, and, through long and weary millennia, be born again from stardust before these lost miracles of the green and blue shall reawaken.

We will think of ways we might keep them from being forever lost from Earth. Yet first, we will meet some of them. Of all the countless ambassadors of the divine from among the fauna, I introduce you to one whose pristine heart is a golden book of wisdom. Let the wise, therefore, read Juliet's open book and be the wiser.

When Juliet was only a few weeks old, her mother was murdered by a lost soul, inebriated upon his frightened ego. He left her and her two cub brothers, no bigger than cherubs, to starve to death in the vast north woods, as so many cubs who are orphaned by hunters do. Yet, the three little siblings were quickly rescued by an old black bear who may have been their grandmother or aunt. She, however, could provide little comfort to the cubs, for, being weak and arthritic, she was scarcely able to care for herself. So, with stiff and painful movements, the old she-bear slowly approached a log cabin, seeking help, where a young man sat on the front porch, for she easily sensed his goodness.

Six feet away from him, she sat on her hind legs and began to weep while fixing her gaze upon the man with desperate, grieving expressions. While pleading in the softest tones, surpassing all barriers of human speech, she then looked upward where terrified little Juliet and her two brothers clung to a tree, high above. Earlier, the man had seen hunters in a boat carrying away a black bear they had just killed, whom he assumed to be the cubs' mother. He understood, more clearly than if the words were spoken in English, that the old bear was imploring the man, with brokenhearted supplications, to care for the cubs. Then the aged matriarch, her face wet with tears, her steps halting and stiff, ambled back into the woods.

The man finally enticed the trio to descend and eat by leaving a savory, sweet-smelling hot meal at the base of the tree, where Juliet and her brothers trembled in fear. Yet, as woefully rheumatic as the old bear was, she had not forgotten the cubs.

"At about six o'clock at every afternoon of that first week, the old bear came to the edge of the forest, called the cubs, held a hasty conference, sent them back to the cabin, then trundled away . . . After the seventh day, we never saw her again."

After several days of leaving his cabin door open, the three timidly tiptoed into the man's home, led by Juliet's courageous big brother, whom I call Brawn Bones. The smallest sibling of the three, the Professor, sheepishly followed Juliet and Brawn. After having devoured a delicious hot meal, the cabin's warmth and the softness of a few old army blankets irresistibly beckoned even these children of the wild. While standing on his hind legs, the Professor analyzed the blankets, tilting his head quizzically to the right, scratching his right ear, then tilting his head to the left, scratching that ear. Yet, without the analytical intellectuality of his little brother, Brawn nuzzled into the blankets, sighing in a deep guttural purr. And with feminine grace and softness apparent even at her baby-doll size, Juliet gingerly snuggled next to him. Then, as if to say, "Oh, well," the Professor joined them. Three pairs of button eyes gazed at the man, then blinked . . . and drooped . . . and though the fight to remain awake was valiant for the three teddy bears, honey-sweet sleep finally won, and they closed their eyes.

A few days passed, and, after the man fed the cubs a big meal of rainbow trout and all were resting by the warmth of the hearth, Brawn walked over to the man and placed his muzzle on his knee. Juliet and the Professor were thus emboldened to touch their new daddy, and soon all three were in his lap. He later wrote, "If nature cheated porcupines, turtles, and armadillos out of any ability to get cuddly, she made up for the deficiency when she created bears. My personal enjoyment of a lapful of cubs every night was no greater than that of the cubs themselves. That first nine days of fear and distance quickly gave way to a passionate urgency to press physically close and have my fingers run constantly through their luxuriant fur when they sat with me on the big willow-bough" chair by the fireplace. "That night, when they first climbed into my lap, they crawled into the roomy down sleeping bag with me. I liked their clean, fresh-straw smell, and their warm little bodies almost compensated for their snoring . . ."

The man quickly learned that black bears share more psychological traits with humans than, perhaps, any other animal. For it seemed as though almost overnight Juliet and her brothers learned valuable lessons the man taught them about foraging for food, manners while inside the cabin, and escaping danger by scampering up a tree when he would clap his hands and shout, "Tree!" Yet, *without* training, Juliet and the boys would walk and even run on their hind legs. Sometimes they would find a curious object and take turns tossing it back and forth to each other in a threesome of catch. And their favorite toys endlessly entertained Juliet and Brawn so much that they often took their toys to bed with them, although toys were somewhat childish for the erudite Professor.

The Professor, however, was not without levity. One night when the man was troubled, the Professor sought to lighten the man's burden. He "would roll, play with his toes, chew a stick of cardwood, or assume ridiculous positions on the floor to flag my attention when I became drowsy. If I dozed, he nibbled my ears; if I failed to register an expression of applause to any of his antics, he repeated the performance until I did."

Such hilarity was part of Juliet's and her brother's lives as they grew and learned and became ever more fascinated by their new adventuresome world. Walks with the man into the deep woods and canoe rides were times of joyous fascination. But one day, when Juliet was about two years old and almost fully grown, the man readied the canoe for a trip across the lake, at which time Brawn and the Professor scampered aboard. Yet, Juliet stopped at the water, refusing to climb in. As the others pulled away from the shore, Juliet turned and disappeared into the forest behind the cabin.

As much as Juliet loved her two brothers and the man,

she discovered something that she felt they could never understand—something that no one could understand. For how could others realize what they have never experienced or even dreamed? This newness of life that beautified every leaf, every pine, the clouds at sunrise, the wildflowers of the meadow, now made all things bright. Now, the why and wherefore were so clear, so easy. And, with this miraculous epiphany, which Juliet felt certain she was the first to ever experience, she sensed her eternalness. For he was wild, weighed over four hundred pounds, and was stronger than seven strong men. Yet, when he placed his paw upon her shoulder, as he was wont to do, his touch was a replication of the delicate tenderness within his heart he felt for only Juliet.

They met every day up on the high trail in a courtship that was to last a year before leading to mating and her own cubs. Yet for now, walking together in the ancient forest and touching were all they could imagine. Bruno, for this name befits his masculinity, would ever so gently lick Juliet across the bridge of her nose, a bear's gesture of dearest affection. Other times they would stand facing one another with their paws on the other's shoulders, each enthralled in the nearness of the other, intensified with the regret of knowing they must part 'til the morrow. Thus, of all the countless ambassadors from among the fauna, 'tis

Juliet's innocent heart that is our golden book of wisdom.[9]

Another member of the fauna is an iridescent vignette, which has been sent to us by our Lord's grace, a ruby-throated hummingbird, the smallest bird of all. His name is Mercury, being herald of spring's sudden arrival in North America and for his ability to fly sixty miles per hour, zipping hither and thither amongst flower and feeder. The nectar he imbibes there is merely jet fuel for his jigsaw, aerobatic pursuit of insects, for he is a voracious carnivore. And he enjoys the advantage of flying backward, the only bird in the world who can perform such a feat. Even so, competition for flies and spiders is intense in his winter home of Central America. So, when springtime arrives further north "with its divine spirit of discontent" where "everything is happy, progressive, and occupied," he seeks food there among fewer rivals. Perhaps, he also seeks a place where he and his mate can nest with their chicks, fearing less threat from predators who might eat their eggs or fledglings. Nevertheless, Mercury befuddles ornithologists with his miraculous flight, which is to them inexplicable, for he ventures three thousand miles to these happier hunting grounds, returning each year to the precise location of his birth.

---

[9] The story of Juliet and Bruno, of Brawn and the Professor is an adaption of *The Bears and I,* the nonfiction book by Robert Franklin Leslie. Although the story I have told is an adaption, I have been careful to not include any fictitious variations but only accurate accounts according to Leslie's record. So, the reader may rest assured that all I have written truly occurred. I have, however, given the bears new names.

Earlier this year, Mercury began flying north in early January, and, by the end of February, he arrived at the northern coast of Yucatan, where he devoured an extra supply of insects and spiders. That added a thick layer of fat needed for warmth and energy during the next leg of his flight to the United States. Some of his cousins who were weaker, older, or timid, followed the coast northward. Yet, Mercury and most of his cousins gathered all their courage to brave the open waters of the Gulf of Mexico. Before departing, he almost doubled his weight to more than six grams. Then, one fair twilight, he set wing to his nonstop, five-hundred-mile flight, which lasted nearly twenty-two hours. When he reached the shores of the United States, tiny yet great-hearted Mercury was exhausted, weighing only 2.4 grams, having expended sixty percent of his body weight during his arduous flight.

His paramour, Atalanta, so named for her racing speed, and all the other females joined him ten days later. Upon resting and having regained their normal weight, his intrepid flock continued migrating at twenty miles each day, following the earliest blooming of their preferred flowers until reaching the various places of their respective births.

Without delay, Atalanta constructed a nest in the shape of a cup with plant materials and spider webs, gluing pieces of lichen to the exterior of her nest for camouflage. Her eggs, which she and Mercury guarded with their very lives, were the size of a green pea, the smallest egg in the world. And, within that most miniature of eggs, were all the iridescent colors of the hummingbird, the resolute fortitude to fly twenty-two hours without rest, the quicksilver flight, the dazzling aerial maneuvers, the homing instincts, and—the ability to perpetuate them to a thousand generations.

The parents knew this quite well. And so, their eggs were immeasurably more precious to them than the rarest jewels. Mercury attracted predators away from the nest with the iridescence of his red throat, flashing as a ruby in the Sun. Atalanta had no such red reflector, and, therefore, predators were less aware of her nest. In twelve to fourteen days, her babies were fully incubated, and in only another fourteen to eighteen days, her chicks became fledglings.

Now, the chicks soar in a thousand gyrations, propelled by wings that flutter sixty times each second. Now, they are the center of the Universe, the Sun itself revolving 'round them. Here, they skyrocket to the highest branch, chattering to their parents below. There, they zoom by the nest in a blur of green. Feelings of invincibility explode within their tiny hearts, beating twenty-one times each second.

Only past the gates of heaven may we know the exuberant joys the chicks experience in their first glittering summer.

Then, as the days shorten, the light of the Sun becoming less and less with the advent of autumn, there comes an irresistible urge to fly south within Mercury's and Atalanta's breasts. Their chicks feel the same involuntary impulse. And, by the middle of July, the new family begins their long, perilous journey to the jungles far away to the south.

Let us now visit an ambassadress of the flora. Outside my bedroom window and balcony lives a giant female pistache tree, her branches stretching forty to fifty feet toward the sky. For the last six years, she has brought me much joy and happiness with her ever-changing beauty of spring-green, to pink, to orange, to bright vermillion in the fall. With her calming presence, there is a high spiritual quality that she has blest me with ten thousand times, more times than I have consciously realized, as I might have caught a glimpse of her while walking by my windows when busy with other things.

She has welcomed many birds who have alighted on her branches, exactly twenty-eight species of whom were encouraged to visit my balcony. Her canopy of many colors gives the smaller birds a place to dash away from predators circling above. Playful squirrels also depend upon her for safety, for their nests, for red berries, and for their rambunctious, dizzy paths along her many branches.

In full bloom, she provides respite from the pounding of the August Sun's anvil, casting shadows in dapples of white-yellow and purple playing gently 'cross the ground beneath her. Countless living wonders buzz and hide in her dense foliage. She gives me privacy, as well, for none can peer into my windows as she dons her breathtaking summer fashion.

A breeze stirs the air from stillness, rustling her leaves, the sunlight causing a metallic shimmering upon each one, reminiscent of a bejeweled jade headdress a great lady might wear, that sparkles and gently beckons. Upon this breeze, she slowly rustles unto exaltation, the sound of her rippling leaves inviting all those around to join her carefree rest. Then, without hurry, she relaxes to halcyon stillness again.

And Queen Caroline, for this is the name I have given her, has a love life among discriminating paramours. Selectively, she only attracts male pistaches, for she wishes to mate exclusively with her species. They woo from far away, whom she delights with the sweetest feminine unctions. Perhaps we will hear these unctuous whispers, spiritual and so splendidly ladylike, when we awaken in heaven. The amorous males send their love letters, entrusted to butterflies, bees, hummingbirds, or a wafting zephyr. Some call this pollination. Yet, isn't it miraculous love? Of course, she gives us and our fellow fauna oxygen to breathe. Yes, without the faithful photosynthesis of Her Majesty and that of the other flora, we would surely suffocate. For she and the other plants of Earth produce all the oxygen that is breathed by the fauna, of which we are but a member. In unconscious reciprocation, the fauna exhales the carbon dioxide that the flora needs for respiration and photosynthesis. In this symbiotic relationship, the flora and fauna are mutually interdependent, the survival of one species, including ours, utterly depending upon the continuation of the other. So, isn't it appropriate to be in awe of Her Majesty, the Queen?

And may I introduce Ginger, who visits me daily to sit on the windowsill by my desk? This pretty little squirrel takes peanuts and apple slices from my hand so gingerly, hence her name. Perhaps I would be remiss should I not also mention Pavarotti, the tiny purple finch whom I have seen and heard on two occasions sing to his mate with the most splendid tenor melodies, inexpressibly tenderhearted and joyous, while swaying from side to side, proclaiming divine love to the wide world. During this serenade, his mate hops over to peck him on the cheek and hops back again. Upon her third kiss, they fly away together.

And what of the pecan trees that, together as a little grove, consciously agree to bear no fruit the year after squirrels took more than the trees deem proper? What of the impossible, three-thousand-mile migration of the monarch butterfly, so delicate yet so capable? What of the high-speed cheetah who accelerates from a standing start to forty-seven miles an hour in a blazing two seconds, then accelerates further to seventy miles an hour, flying midair twenty-two feet in a single stride? Let us humble ourselves before these divine missives, for they have come unto this temporal world bearing witness to that which is far more truthful, far more beautiful. Only then shall we stand on the threshold of being their good stewards.

Yet, how have we received these splendid messengers whom the King of Life himself has so graciously sent to us as a token of his love? Since the year A.D. 1600, according to systemic fossil analysis, we have been snuffing them out with disinterested blasphemy—much faster than the normal rate of extinction. Crucial ecosystems are predicted to experience rapid degradation and collapse, with the foreboding prospect of another thirty percent of the flora and fauna disappearing before the year 2100. Many ecologists feel our fate is irretrievable. Moreover, a unifying plan has not been accepted to intercept and halt this blitzkrieg that we wage upon ourselves and all living things upon the Earth. Nonetheless, dear friends, there is one overarching equation that can stop this global death knell that, day after day, peals ever louder.

We will now consider this redeeming equation in a general discussion and then with its algebraic expression, which is quite simple and easily understood.

Chapter Two

Earthly Balance

FIRST of all, I will stress that I believe our future shall be heretofore unsurpassed by all human achievements, the greatest of these being the assumption of our proper place amongst life on Earth. Should this seem an idealistic oversimplification, I am quite aware of the colossal change it implies. It shall require extraordinary work to implement, particularly the work needed to change antiquated thinking. With this thought in mind, let us remember that all problems are solved by work. And we few who are the molders and sculptors of change have never been afraid of hard, smart work, especially its highest form, thoughtwork, which has been and shall continue to be our redemption. So, let us begin.

I will provide only four solutions that answer the divine summons given to us, for once accepted, along with the sheer necessity of mankind's desperate plight, a plethora of supporting solutions will follow them in auto-catalytic fashion, self-perpetually.

Influencing Popular Opinion

The first of these solutions is to position ourselves to sway popular opinion, for this is the crown jewel of our struggle. This, we must master. To be sure, he who controls the media controls all. Therefore, some of the brightest among us must become social scientists who sway the masses with benevolence as their moral compass—its true north ever pointing to nature. Such a feat has become more practical with the maturation of the internet. Yet, our influence must broaden, must deepen into publishing, theater, art, music, and above all—public education.

As we go about these varied tasks, we may be encouraged that opinions shared by only three percent of the masses are enough to sway and then lead the other ninety-seven percent. So, worldviews that redeem us from our headlong descent into existential disaster, sweeping all Earthly[10] life along with it, may be achieved with surpris-

---

[10] The word "Earthly" is an adjective that is not typically capitalized; however, I have taken the poetic freedom to do so throughout this book purely from a respect of all that the word represents.

ing speed and efficiency by like-minded people. For opinion based upon ice-cold fact is the perfect antidote to ecological collapse. As the sudden and unclouded brilliance of an early spring day melts ice and snow into water that rushes from the alpine summit, so do facts slowly melt these antiquated ideas. Of course, there shall be terrific resistance from many corners, likened to a drowning man flailing in wild-eyed terror against his heroic savior. And so, along with its market penetration, acceptance, and the transformation of its ideas into real-world practicality, the materialization of our plan in only a world region or two will take decades. Yet, as the next three decades transpire, at the end of which billions of additional people shall live upon Earth, pent-up demand for a solution will escalate. This may be especially true in more advanced societies, which have become one international incubator, percolating with hundreds of millions of individuated frustrations over many issues that will no longer accept silence.

This book is both conduit and relief valve for their voices. These emancipated words and conversations being shared person to person, multiplying organically, will influence public opinion, allowing us to introduce the equation's remaining subsets. For, to many people, they may seem entirely incompatible with and estranged from contemporary society, *and indeed, they are.* However, its societal incongruity is appropriate, for these notions come to us from a foreign plane—the future yet unvisited. There, in the future, these solutions will become the choice over a socio-economic dynamic that has a tendency toward slavery, wars without end, and the reprobate mind that irresistibly degrades the ecosystem unto collapse.

Now, our equation shall not be enforced by law, a counterproductive supposition and, of course, an impossibility except under the auspices of tyranny, which would be antithetical to the equation itself. As Adam Smith so aptly taught us in his economic masterpiece, *The Wealth of Nations,* prosperity is created across every social stratum of a nation as its citizens are protected by fundamental laws yet free from government meddling, regulations, and over-taxation. Likewise, the equation will yield the highest benefits without coercion, but in a society where an individual may speak his mind without fear, which is freedom's hallmark. Indeed, the same principles of a free-market economy that drive robust commerce will be used to influence individuals to consider the equation's wide-ranging benefits. For example, there are no laws forcing people to buy a luxury home or a vacation in Hawaii. Without such laws, people are extremely motivated to purchase them because these items relieve the pressure of the human condition, which sometimes seems unbearable.

In like manner, the equation will be presented as a free-choice alternative to crime-oppressed neighborhoods, cities, and nations, an alternative to individual and national economic depression. It will offer peace where once was war, a well-educated population where once was illiteracy, prevailing good health where there was chronic disease, advanced social dynamics wherein a sublime civilized life is enjoyed in place of human degradation, and the fluorescence of nature rather than our present appointment with ecological collapse.

And so, the equation will be an advent of higher social norms, mores, and taboos. This shall require time. Perhaps, it will require fifty to seventy-five years. But time shall pass nonetheless, so the prudent soul will wisely use the time we yet have.

Plant-Based Diet

Simultaneously, as we take command of and overcome the popular opinion challenge, our idyllic epoch will truly begin when the bright news is heralded throughout the Earth that the veritable last slaughterhouse has once and forever closed. Besides ending the unspeakable horrors and misery that unfolds there in 56 billion agonizingly long nightmares each year, which is the number of animals slaughtered annually around the world, the Earth's resources will change. The quality of our water and food will materially improve. Fields and forests that calm human fears and give us fresh air will expand and flourish; the diverse wildlife who depends upon these woodlands will rebound. These are the reasons:

One person who eats only the amount of beef in a MacDonald's Quarter Pounder (approximately 4 oz.) every day for 75 years expends the following resources:

• 38,872,500 gallons of water.[11]
Bovines need a significant amount of water for drinking, irrigating, and other needs. This number represents the water necessary to produce only 4.4 oz. of beef multiplied over 75 years (1,420 gallons for 4.4 oz. of beef x 75 yrs. = 38,872500 gallons).

• 47 tons of grain.[12]
Grain farming for livestock feed requires the clearing of life-giving flora. To produce 4.375 oz. of beef, an average of 3 lbs. 7 oz. (3.45 lbs.) of grain is required (3.45 lbs. daily x 75 yrs. = 94,443.75 lbs. ÷ 2000 lbs. = 47.22 tons)

---

[11] David Pimentel, Bonnie Berger, David Filiberto, Michelle Newton, Benjamin Wolfe, Elizabeth Karabinakis, Steven Clark, Elaine Poon, Elizabeth Abbett, Sudha Nandagopal, *Water Resources: Agricultural and Environmental Issues,* (Oxford: Oxford University Press, 2004) volume 54, issue 10, pages 909–918
[12] J. L. P., "Meats and greens; How bad for the planet is eating meat?" (London: The Economist, 2013)

• 5,365,500 square feet of field and forest. [13]

The figure above represents the loss of field and forest caused by eating 4 ounces of beef over 75 years. (4 oz. of beef requires 196 sq. ft. daily x 75 yrs. = 5,365,500 sq. ft. or 123 acres).

"The livestock sector is by far the single largest anthropogenic user of land. The total area occupied by grazing is equivalent to 26 percent of the ice-free terrestrial surface of the planet. In addition, the total area dedicated to feedcrop production amounts to 33 percent of total arable land. In all, livestock production accounts for 70 percent of all agricultural land and 30 percent of the land surface of the planet."[14]

• As we continue the theme of the 75-year carnivorous diet, we discover that individuals consume an average of 2,250 mammals and over 2 tons of fish in the U.S. This is because almost 10 billion animals and nearly 9 million tons of fish are slaughtered in the United States each year.[15] [16] (9,812,386,000 animals slaughtered in the U.S.

---

[13] Rosi, A., Mena, P., Pellegrini, N. et al. "Environmental impact of omnivorous, ovo-lacto-vegetarian, and vegan diet," (New York: Scientific Reports, 2017)

[14] *Livestock's Long Shadow; Environmental Issues and Options,* (Rome: FAO of the United Nations, 2006)

[15] *Livestock & Meat Domestic Data, Livestock and Poultry Slaughter,*

annually ÷ 327,167,000 U.S. pop. = 30 animals butchered annually per capita x 75 yrs. = 2,250). (55 lbs. of fish consumed annually per capita in the U.S. x 75 yrs. = 4,133 lbs. or 2 tons, 133 lbs.)

Zero mercy is given to most of these animals, especially during transport to the slaughterhouse as they are shipped in filthy trucks where the smaller of the doomed are crushed to death by others who cannot move in the cram-packed conditions. Sometimes, this trip to hell occurs in freezing temperatures, other times, in heatwaves. Their inability to move prevents them from warming themselves, seeking shade, or even a gasp of air in days of sweltering heat. Precious few are killed humanely.

The irony is astonishing since this indescribable misery is permitted billions of times each year so that humans can supposedly enjoy better health. However, a "large body of evidence has shown that higher red meat consumption, especially processed red meat, is associated with an increased risk of type 2 diabetes, cardiovascular disease, certain types of cancer, including colorectal can-

---

(Washington, DC: United States Department of Agriculture, 2019)
[16] *The State of World Fisheries and Aquaculture 2018 - Meeting the*

sustainable development goals. (Rome: FAO of the United Nations, 2018)

cer, and mortality. Consumption of processed red meat (e.g., bacon, hot dogs, and sausages) has been associated with additional health outcomes, including chronic obstructive pulmonary disease, heart failure, and hypertension."[17] It is not surprising, therefore, that the risk of colon cancer is increased 16% by eating only 50 grams of processed meat daily, about the equivalent of one hot dog.[18] Consequently, The World Health Organization's International Agency for Research on Cancer has stated that consumption of red meat is "probably carcinogenic" to humans, but processed meat is *definitely* "carcinogenic."[19]

While slaughterhouses are dens of wretched privations, dairy farms may be less merciful. Here, cows are forcibly impregnated by artificial means, which is painful and, let there be no question about it, rape. After nine months of pregnancy, the same term as humans, they give birth. Yet, the babies receive none of their mother's milk. It is stolen from both mother and baby and purchased as

---

[17] *Association of changes in red meat consumption with total and cause-specific mortality among US women and men: two prospective cohort studies*, (London: British Medical Journal, 2019)
[18] "Processed Meats Increase Colorectal Cancer Risk, New Report," (Arlington: American Institute for Cancer Research, 2017)
[19] "Q&A on the carcinogenicity of the consumption of red meat and processed meat," (Geneva: The World Health Organization, 2015)

though it was a product. But the unwitting consumers might be reluctant to participate in this monstrous cruelty if they knew what is behind their purchase at the local grocer.

The traumatic loss to mothers of their babies is evidenced by bemoaning cries, an eerie bewailing that lasts for days after their babies are stolen and haunts each dairy farm every nine months.

Bull calves are dumped in a wheelbarrow and carted away to be slaughtered for veal for no other reason than that diners may prefer a softer texture to their meat. Cow calves are taken to a tiny, sequestered area where they are fattened and injected with growth hormones and, as soon as they can give birth, raped by artificial insemination.

And so, the cycle of misery continues. All this so that humans can drink and eat various forms of animal milk, which medical research has linked to cancer, diabetes, gastrointestinal inflammation, cognitive impairment,[20] multiple sclerosis, deadly microorganisms, high concen-

----

[20] Jianqin, S., Leiming, X., Lu, X. et al. Effects of milk containing only A2 beta-casein versus milk containing both A1 and A2 beta casein-proteins on gastrointestinal physiology, symptoms of discomfort, and cognitive behavior of people with self-reported intolerance to traditional cows' milk. Nutr J 15, 35 (2015) doi:10.1186/s12937-016-0147-z

trations of pesticides, and antibiotic residues.[21]

Is it easy to break the habit of eating animal flesh and blood and selfishly consuming various forms of milk intended by nature for their babies? Yes, it is, dear friends, for doing so is moral, humane, and only a change of mindset.

Those who make this transformation discover that a purer, more potent source of protein and vitamin B-12 is available without animal flesh or their milk and the health threats they pose. One vitamin B-12 capsule and 60 grams of protein powder, for example, are far more beneficial than eating a steak. Moreover, by using these supplements, their amounts can be measured precisely for optimal well-being and vitality. Combined with fresh organic vegetables, fruits, grains, and nuts, they improve our appearance, energy, strength, *and the way we think*, leading to a heightened sense of awareness, which is the single gateway to world change.

Begin by eating only organic food that is free from pesticides and preservatives. With very few exceptions, avoid processed food or food that is not as it grew in its natural state. Buying a blender is also advisable; it needn't be expensive but should hold about six cups. Start your

---

[21] Ochoa, Sofia Pineda, M.D., *7 Ways Milk and Dairy Products Are Making You Sick,* (Los Angeles: Forks Over Knives, 2016)

day with zest by blending delicious smoothies, rich with life-giving foods such as kale, spinach, blueberries, and strawberries for breakfast. You might enjoy a bowl of oatmeal after this for enduring strength and energy throughout the day. Try a big salad for lunch with a bountiful supply of various colored vegetables, especially those that are dark green and leafy. Sprinkle it with olive oil and apple cider vinegar. Dinner is limited only by your imagination. You might try a green bell pepper stuffed with brown rice, green peas, corn, tomato paste, and enriched with olive oil. A red bell pepper prepared with the same ingredients but mixed with avocado, rather than tomato paste, is a different-colored version of the same idea (a few more recipes are presented later in this book). After a week of eating this way, you'll be invigorated with positive energy extending to the world around you.[22]

Earthly Cities and Transportation

Let's go forward in time to meet Dane, one of our progenies, and observe his trip to see his fiancé in the next city.

From home, he rides his bike to the nearby turnstile,

---

[22] Always consult you physician before staring a new diet. And, remember, the plant-based diet must be supplemented with high-quality vegan protein powder and vitamin B-12.

where Strauss's *Myrtle Blossom Waltz* is playing upon his arrival. Although most passengers only hear its sublime harmony subconsciously, it creates a relaxed but cheery ambiance in tune with the spring morning.

In two snaps, he secures his bike in the public bike locks and bounds down the stairs and through the turnstile's wide gates, where he purchases his fare on his wrist computer. In a few minutes, he's aboard, comfortably seated, and silently levitating at an average destination speed of 243 miles per hour. Dane inhales deeply and exhales with a sigh that bespeaks of his hurried bike ride. He sets his backpack against the side of the carriage and, using it as a pillow, leans on it, folds his arms, and thinks of Ingrid's smile.

His eyes close, his head nods. Suddenly, he feels the train halt. He awakens to see the other passengers disembarking. "Thirty-one minutes," he mumbles while forcing his eyes open with a few blinks. Grabbing his backpack, he dashes out the carriage door and onto the turnstile. Casually walking toward the gate, he looks about and stops in the yellow spotlight of Sun beaming there, whereupon he feels a tap on his shoulder. Spinning around, he sees the face of which he just dreamt.

"What took you so long?" Ingrid asks with a teasing smile.

They hug, they kiss. She takes the picnic basket off her shoulder. They kiss, they hug. "Wait!" Ingrid says with mild alarm. "If we don't hurry, you'll miss the last rental bike!"

Dane takes her hand, leading the way as they run up the stairs into the sunlight, which causes their involuntary laughter for reasons well known to lovers. At the top of the steps, they pause in unexpected unison as if about to walk into a place sacred, causing their natural reverence.

The green cathedral with its vaulted columns of thick bark evokes feelings of children standing before venerated parents, so tall, so high above. Ingrid draws close to Dane and puts her arm in his. They stand in hushed awe, unwilling to violate the sanctity of this sublime moment.

The forest air is blessedly pure. They breathe deeply, look at each other, smile, and share one soft little kiss.

Without speaking, Dane rents his bicycle with a sweep of his wrist computer while Ingrid waits on her bike in the dirt trail just wide enough for a bike or two, either side being thick with wild growth. Huge sunflowers, towering above tall Dane and opened with yellow rejoicings, wave gently to and fro.

As they ride along, two cottontail rabbits sit on the trail before them, watching them curiously. Then, with their white tails betraying their escape, zip to the left, dart to the right, then disappear in the thicket. Further down the trail, squirrels chatter overhead in a heated issue. A possum rests indifferently on his belly, his legs hanging on either side of a tree limb they ride beneath. A mockingbird sings a rendition of his ancient songs and flies from limb to branch as though welcoming, escorting them for a hundred feet or so.

Pedaling for another twenty minutes, they approach *Swan Lake,* where, in the far distance below, they see Ingrid's mother busy with her picnic feast spread on a blanket before her. Her father is down by the water where he waits for Brian, the family's wooly retriever, who splashes back to shore with reckless abandon with his stick. From the distance, they faintly hear Brian's splashing in contrast to the quietness by the lake. It appears the birds and others have taken a midmorning break.

Dane and Ingrid stop at the crest of the overlooking hill to take in the welcoming scene. After a few moments, she says, "Look, Dane. Over there by the trail—a bronze sign." They walk their bikes over to take a closer look, and he reads the words aloud:

"For over half a century, this forest was buried beneath sprawling asphalt parking lots, an eight-lane highway to the southwest, and an international airport to the east. Today, it is rich with blossoming life of over one thousand species of flora and over two hundred species of birds. Now, deer, antelopes, buffalos, bison, black bears, wolves, coyotes, cougars, and mountain lions roam twenty miles from the picnic grounds in the deep woods and vast prairies far beyond.

"Never again shall we bury God's gift."

This story is based on an epiphany I received one morning while running along the river trail by my home, as I always do around daybreak. Previously, there was only one trail, yet this was somehow inconvenient. A bureaucrat deemed that a second trail must be built, for this would be an "improvement," allowing cyclists and runners to have their respective paths.

Now two trails run parallel for miles. The new trail, however, was built over one-quarter mile of sunflowers, many of which stood seven feet and higher, opening their bright yellow solar panels unto the Sun. They seemed to smile and cheer me, a greeting beyond price, and I responded involuntarily with a smile. I feel there must have been some awareness within those yellow sunbursts, unexplained by science a knowing. Yet now, along with many other wild trees and shrubs that once grew tall and beautiful, they are entombed 'neath asphalt in cold darkness.

The thought flashed before me of the myriad forms of once blossoming life buried under millions upon millions of acres of concrete and asphalt in our megacities, where nary a green shoot is allowed. I thought of the superhighways inlaid into our Earth in crisscross networking, creating a lifeless swath one-quarter mile wide for hundreds of miles in every direction, suffocating the green miracles that give every living thing its next breath.

Let us find an objective means to judge this morass of "improvements," a way to truly understand these monstrosities we call cities. Perhaps, we could find such objectivity from an honest heart, a heart that has never sinned. Is there such a one among us?

A viewpoint from the heavens might be obtained. In this case, 'tis a view from a bluebird whose ancestors not so long ago adorned our skies in abundance with beauty and song. What jolt of debilitating horror must grip the blameless heart of this little bird fluttering desperately over a megacity that seems bereft of any living thing save numb humans who embrace and cower before the non-living, slaving for things inanimate.

Here, this precious soul, desperate in its innocence, finds few trees to alight upon and fewer sources of food and water. What horror for the little bird to behold this corpse-gray absence of life. The air, dense with carbon monoxide, chokes his flock, and the others fall upon the pavement.

Now alone, his angelic heart torn asunder from grief, this winging refugee can fly no more and lands upon a building, panting frantically, confused. The long day bakes the concrete and glass, waning slowly unto afternoon, unto evening, hot and brutal. If just a single drop of water . . . if only one morsel.

Finally, the Sun sets, and this brings some hope of repose—of quietness—so that he might gain some strength through sleep. But even the sacred night is violated with a glaring artificial glow that penetrates his blessed closed eyes, his ears with blasting traffic blare, unmerciful in its incessancy. The little bluebird, aghast that anything could be this horrid, loses the will to live and, with a winged beauty perfected, is taken, is taken far, far away to sweet freedom.

Are these cities, and the vast grid of streets and thoroughfares leading through and around them, in any way attuned to nature?

Now, to seek another objective understanding of our cities, and also our towns and countrysides, let us suppose a towering giant stood before all the people of Earth and, in a loud and terrible voice, shouted, "I offer you the ability to move about your cities and across your land effortlessly. But you must slave and suffer trauma for this.

"What is more, to earn my provision, although you must work and labor for it, I will yet require the lives of no less than 5 billion animals each year, horribly killing and mangling them without mercy as a sacrifice unto me. I shall do the same to members of your family, killing over 1 million of them year after year. I shall crisscross your fields and meadows with death-gray concrete and steel where once life blossomed and rejoiced. I shall destroy your virgin forests, leaving no living thing in their place.

"Now, people of Earth, if you refuse, I shall go away never to return, leaving you in peace.

"But should you accept my offer, know that you must slave and labor for my gift. And remember that I shall slaughter and murder as I please, whomsoever I please, taking 5 billion lives each year of the perfectly innocent fauna. Neither should you fail to remember that I shall mow down your fields and forests and meadows leaving death in place of their blooming life. I shall brutally kill over 1 million humans each year. I shall maim and cripple many, many more. For this, people of Earth, I shall give you ease of transportation."

Of course, the people of Earth would never accept such a nightmarish offer, would they? Perhaps, we would. For I have just described the bargain we make with transportation technology to drive cars, although doing so viciously kills an estimated *5 billion* fauna each and every year.[23] And, ever more roads and highways are demanded

---

[23] Approximately 1.3 million animals die every day after having been struck by cars and trucks in Brazil where 80 million automobiles are in operation; thus, reports the Centro Brasileiro de Estudos em Ecologia de Estradas in a recent study. This is a ratio of 1.3 percent of motor vehicles to animal related deaths. Such studies are not readily available in other countries. Yet, at the risk of extrapolation, should we apply Brazil's ratio of 1.3 to the 1.2 billion cars around the globe, we see that 5.7 billion animals are killed each year by cars.

by the people of Earth to drive their cars over the once blessed forests, fields, and meadows where life once blossomed but now lay entombed 'neath concrete and asphalt. Although over 1 million humans[24] are also indiscriminately killed and many more injured each year, this is the bargain we have made.

How might we escape enslavement from this terrible giant ogre with his morbid demands?

The elegant response to this question is *subterranean travel*. Underground transportation has been employed successfully for many years with train systems such as the Moscow Metro, the New York Subway, the Paris Metro, and the London Underground, which together transport 7 billion riders each year, the equivalent of Earth's human population. Of these four, all of which I have traveled upon, the Moscow Metro is the largest and most beautiful, its spacious pathways luxurious with art and chandeliers.

The travelers who use these systems, and many others around the world, are unencumbered by storms, rain, snow, and excessive heat. Neither their lives nor their safety are threatened by reckless drivers, and they do not lose time in traffic jams. They also save money. Travel within these subterranean systems allows them to avoid the significant cost of purchasing a car, fuel costs, routine

---

[24] Global Health Observatory, (Geneva: The World Health Organization, 2013)

and unexpected maintenance, car accidents, car insurance, traffic fines, parking fees, and possible legal fees, court time, and lawsuits. They avoid the trauma associated with keeping up with these costs, as well as trauma from driving itself, particularly in heavy traffic. Car theft, burglaries, and vandalism are also eliminated. And, the greatest benefit of all, they have removed themselves from the grasp of the horrible giant, who mercilessly kills over 1 million people each year and grievously injures many more.

Furthermore, they do not contribute to the deaths of over 5 billion animals year after year or the ever increasing, wanton destruction of our forests, fields, meadows, and streams.

The sensibility of subterranean travel is compelling. It may prove to be faster and more convenient than air travel. Technology presently exists in which passenger cars magnetically levitate above a track and are electrically propelled through a low-pressure tube at almost 700 miles per hour. Upon the completion of a network of these underground tubes, air travel may seem quite antique.

Some of the staunchest resistance to these ideas may come from industries such as oil, automotive manufacturers, car insurance, and highway construction. Yet, let them not make the same mistake made by the railroad captains of industry, who thought of themselves as strictly "railroad men" rather than travel industrialists. Although the railroads had ample funding to begin the first national and international airway companies, their narrow thinking allowed air travel pioneers to take the lion's share of their business from them. Likewise, should they have the foresight to embrace it, the economic bonanza of subterranean travel awaits the world's industrial leaders.

Another point of resistance will undoubtedly be those who love the autonomy of car ownership, which is especially profound in the United States. This is not a negative critique but simply a positive observation that helps us understand the viewpoint and feelings of others. These are two of the most prominent reasons resistance will be found in America: first, when the country was new, between 1862 and 1934, the federal government gave 160 acres, then 360 acres, and finally 640 acres to those who would settle the land granted to them in return for farming and producing crops. Implicit within the grant was the willingness to endure locust and mosquito plagues, drought, scorching heat, sub-zero arctic blasts, lawlessness, crop failure, hunger, endless labor, barren loneliness, and other heavy hardships.

Nevertheless, thousands of rough and ready settlers answered the call and were granted over 270 million acres, almost ten percent of the entire country. This windfall, given to mostly poor people, was religiously fueled by the notion of Genesis 1:28. "Be fruitful, and multiply, and replenish the earth, and subdue it: and have dominion over the fish of the sea, and over the fowl of the air, and over every living thing that moveth upon the earth." Indeed, taming the West was wild and fast and fiercely independent, a prevailing mentality that is, at once, both vice and virtue among Americans today.

The second reason notable resistance will be encountered in the United States is merely that automobile use and American cities grew simultaneously. Consequently, American cities were designed for car travel. They were, therefore, spread across expansive areas, whereas towns of the early American colonies and Europe were designed for walking, horseback riding, carriages, and wagons. By contrast, cars require substantially more space with their parking lots, thoroughfares, and superhighways. And so, the resulting urban and suburban sprawl challenges most Americans who wish to live without a car.

However, private cars propelled along a rail system with the same magnetic levitation described previously might be used underground, thus allowing embarkation near our homes rather than mass transit turnstiles that may be too far to walk or ride a bicycle. One of the challenges of privately-owned subterranean cars is the varied level of maintenance that private ownership implies. This could be overcome quite easily should our cars be provided as a public utility while retaining our prerogative to choose the level of quality we wish, leasing annually, or renting for shorter terms. Thus, the uniformity of performance would be assured.

Of course, anything that is mechanical can and will break down, and such a breakdown could cause hours of delay in these roadway tubes. So, along with the rails for them to travel upon, parallel service rails would be mandatory in this scenario just as they are in our present subway systems.

Subterrestrial cars might have the ability to travel independently during short trips at speeds slightly exceeding those of a golf cart. Yet, when entering a larger underground thoroughfare, they would connect with a laser or, perhaps, a hardware connection in a train-like system, a technology that has existed for several decades prior to this writing. Upon connection to other cars traveling in train-like fashion, speed would increase significantly. Traveling underground in this train-like manner will sharply reduce energy since they will use fuel uniformly in accordance with their respective itineraries. Moreover, because there will be a reduced drag coefficient as the cars travel through a controlled atmosphere in which they do not encounter wind turbulence, they will require even less energy.

This futuristic travel will also save considerable time since, as we have mentioned, subterranean cars will travel in systemic coordination with one another, thereby avoiding traffic delays. These cars traveling in train-mode will drive in perfect harmony with traffic laws, reducing accidents to a fraction of the incidence experienced in surface vehicles, saving many or all of the more than 1 million lives lost by their use.

Pedestrian injuries and deaths will also be virtually eliminated since no pedestrian pathways will exist underground except for short walkways from limited parking places (in the rare case of private train car ownership), to stairs, escalators, or elevators. Private train cars, along with subterranean mass transit, will save our fauna since they will enjoy their habitat without human, automobile, or roadway encroachment or contact. Consequently, as we have seen, this system will save the lives of over 5 billion animals struck and killed by cars globally each year.

And, our communities will be *utterly* free from all vehicle and roadway noise. Rather than the roar of engines, sirens, and tire-to-pavement noise, we will hear the sweet morning rejoicing of birds, the wind rustling the trees, and maybe a nearby stream that was previously hidden by an overpass, which was long ago removed.

Like the bright and beautiful Moscow Metro, these caverns shall be animated with light. Natural sunlight might be intensified by mirror reflection and directed to illuminate, and possibly heat, the cavern highways and byways. Fresh air could be drawn in and out by shafts with little need for energy consumption. Stairs, escalators, and elevators will lead to businesses, homes, and parks above. These common turnstiles, where thousands will pass day and night, will be made safe to a large degree by merely piping classical music to speakers located within and around them. For the tonal resonance of a classic masterpiece is attuned to those in harmony with society, whereas it is received as a discomforting dissonance by social malcontents such as drug dealers, prostitutes, thieves, and other predators, consistently discouraging their presence.[25]

Having described privately operated subterrestrial cars as well as publicly shared subterrestrial trains, we should be mindful that the later is preferred by those seeking Earthly balance for its superior efficiency.

Now, how might Earthly cities be designed? We have just laid the groundwork for them by eliminating terrestrial vehicles, for the cities of the future will no longer be planned for surface automobiles, as they are today. With the additional space once used for cars (which will be considerable), gardens can be planted, and the wilderness allowed to thrive for the relaxation and enjoyment of

---

[25] "5 things to know about fighting crime with classical music," (Washington, D.C.: PoliceOne.com, 2018)

those who live and work in these living, smaragdine cit-ies, just as Dane and Ingrid will enjoy them. Ivy and other climbing flora will adorn the sides of buildings where possible. Grass, shrubs, and trees will be atop buildings, as well, which is presently being done to some degree in a few cities.

Yet, when it becomes the norm, our cities will be cooler, calmer, and naturally inviting to office building tenants and residents alike. These Earthly cities will continue to be occupant dense with vertical growth when possible but within reason. In this way, the city shall be the city, the countryside shall be countryside, with bright delineation between the two. In other words, city dwellers will be able to go for a walk and picnic in an old-growth forest in the morning, walking back to their apartment or condominium by mid-afternoon. Those who make their home in the suburbs will live within forests, fields, near rivers and streams; like city dwellers, they will enjoy utter freedom from traffic noise.

Overpopulation

I introduce blessed Nidhi in this section, the beautiful girl to whom this book is most reverently dedicated. For, as you will see, her unforgettable tale intertwines with disproportional world demographics.

First, let us think about the urgent matters that assail

her and each of us surreptitiously as a thief in the night.

We can wait no longer to begin our return to Eden, for some ecologists estimate that humans use the equivalent resources of 1.7 Earths each year.[26] Because of this consuming onslaught, stunningly sudden in the context of our planet's unhurried evolution, many scientists believe Earth is amid a sixth epochal extinction, the last of which was the fifth episode that annihilated the dinosaurs 65 million years ago. Indeed, the flora and fauna, upon which all life depends, are disappearing at almost inconceivable speeds. Worldwide, more than 56 billion farmed animals[27] and over 90 million tons of fish[28] are slaughtered each year in the most unmerciful ways. And as we have seen, an estimated 5 billion animals are struck and killed by cars each year. Humans are clearing the forests at the

---

[26] According to overshootday.org, "Earth Overshoot Day marks the date when we (all of humanity) have used more from nature than our planet can renew in the entire year. We are using 1.7 Earths. We use more ecological resources and services than nature can regenerate through overfishing, overharvesting forests, and emitting more carbon dioxide into the atmosphere than ecosystems can absorb."

[27] Rowland, Michael Pellman, "11 Facts About Your Food that Will Shock You," (Jersey City: Forbes, 2017)

[28] *2018 The State of the World Fisheries and Aquaculture*, (Rome: Food and Agriculture Organization of the United Nations, 2018)

rate of 40 football fields every minute.[29] Our skies, once a symphony with the songs of wild birds, are now dull and quiet, as only ten percent of the former flocks remain. Huge flocks once winged across the blue dome of heaven, stretching for miles, hurrying along their wide river of serpentine fluttering, and this seamlessly for an hour. I watched this spectacle one autumn day many years ago. But no more. Alas, one half of all the world's wildlife has been lost in the last forty-seven years from this writing; another thirty-percent is predicted to be lost in the coming thirty years. What shall be left of these emissaries who were sent to us with their message of hope?

Much of this rabid rampage derives from over-population, which came upon our life-giving Earth with dizzying momentum. Indeed, when hunter-gatherers became agriculturists, about 8000 B.C., the human population of the world was approximately 5 million. Over the next eight thousand years, ending in approximately A.D. 1, the population grew to 200 million at a rate of less than one-half of one percent each year. At this pace, it took one thousand eight hundred years for the world's population to reach 1 billion (A.D. 1800). The second billion, how-

---

[29] "The World Lost 40 Football Fields of Tropical Trees Every Minute in 2017," (New Haven: Yale School of Forestry and Environmental Studies, 2018)

ever, was realized in only one hundred thirty years (1930), the third billion in thirty years (1960), the fourth billion in fourteen years (1974), and the fifth billion in a mere thirteen years (1987). Effectively, all this geometric growth occurred in less developed countries.[30]

Based upon an analysis of historical and forecasted growth from 1950 to 2050, we see that the developed countries have maintained, and will continue to maintain, a very consistent population, from slightly less than 1 billion in 1950 to a little over 1 billion in 2050. By blatant contrast, the populations of the less developed countries have exploded exponentially from around 3 billion in 1950 to a projected 10 billion in 2050.[31] Indeed, it is predicted that *97% of all population growth will occur in poorer countries.*[32]

Sub-Saharan Africa is the most problematic because this region's population will double or more by 2050[33] and reach over 4 billion by 2100.[34] That is principally because the typical woman there has five children, and their

---

[30] "The Origin of Civilization," (Pasadena: The Saylor Foundation, 2012)

[31] Raleigh, Veena Soni,"Trends in world population: how will the millennium compare with the past?" (Surry: National Institute of Epidemiology, 1999)

[32] "97% of population growth to be in developing world," (London: Consultancy.uk, 2015)

[33] "World Population Prospects: The 2017 Revision," (New York: United Nations, 2017)

[34] UN Population Division Population Projections, (Seattle: Bill and Melinda Gates Foundation, 2017)

children will probably have an average of five children, not because she necessarily wants them, but because procreating is a façade of manhood in that culture.

This accelerating steamroller of egocentricities is predicted to build momentum as the population of these poorer nations geometricizes, rushing toward exhaustion of food, depletion of oxygenating flora, their masses at war for water, for morsels of sustenance. Will the resulting plague and famine overflow into modern cities until their citizens, too, countenance the starving child ever reaching out with an empty hand? Perhaps, this time there shall be nothing left to give. Shall this be our fate? Perhaps, it shall if we continue expending 1.7 Earths annually and more.

But it shall not be our fate, contingent upon the implementation of ideas that are radically different from those we have ever before considered in all the long procession of the human experiment. Conventionality of thought regarding the flora and fauna, of which we are but members, must become preattuned to a death knell—*our* death knell—and this by conditioning at home, a feat possible as only three percent of the population behaves with one mind. Yes, the common and base notions that we are set apart from, over and above the flora and fauna, that we are exceptions to these lives who are perfectly yielded unto nature, that we dwell outside the Realm Instinctive, must become as alien as the plasticine barriers we have built against "the call of the wild."

'Tis a call we must answer with two replies at once: ice-cold rationality and romantic passion; the first, an intonation of the conscious mind wherein reason reigns; the second, the unconscious doorway, the passageway wherein there exists no concept of impossibility. I am quite certain that this philosophy, or *rational romanticism* as I call it, was the mind-set that catapulted the Athenians to the starry heavens, where none have yet to follow. Now, we are poised to pioneer past them unto vastness of virgin soil, rich and loamy, wherein shall be our redeemed world.

Why? Because we must. Middle things are over. The prophet's cry of warning must not be heralded in vain. It must be heeded. For are we not likened to a man blindfolded, standing upon the edge of a precipice with the full knowledge he cannot remain standing there immobile for long, yet also knowing that any blind step may plunge him into a bottomless abyss? Let him fling aside the blindfold to behold the crystalline evidence and step toward safety. Let him do so now.

For the present mindset that is responsible for creating the world's socio-economic system has accepted not only the degradation of the environment but also slavery. This is especially the case in Asia, where sixty percent of the world's population resides as expendable workers and, therefore, where slavery is common. The United Nations Population Fund says, "A doubling of the population in the least developed countries means that between now and 2050 the working-age population will increase by about 15 million persons per year, on average, and that the labor force will increase by 33 thousand persons per day."

These figures are a harbinger of slave labor, and, mixed with the prevailing poverty of the Asiatic nations, they are alarming. China, for example, has a Gross National Product equivalent to the United States but four times the population, thus generally indicating that the average Chinese citizen possesses only twenty-five percent of the wealth enjoyed by each American. However, there are 89 to nearly 92 million members of the Chinese Communist Party with financial privileges, to which their 1.4 billion Chinese fellow citizens are forbidden.[35] [36] So, we see that these demographic explosions create individual poverty and slave labor conditions that will become more frequent and less humane with continued overpopulation.

And in similar less developed nations, there are presently wars without end, raging pestilences, oppressive tyrannies of the inauspicious masses, and an Earth rav-

---

[35] Wong, Chun Han, "China plans to consolidate regulators in sweeping government overhaul," (New York: Wall Street Journal, 2018)

[36] Albert, Maizland, Xu, "The Chinese Communist Party," (New York: Council on Foreign Relations, 2021)

aged beyond repair—horrors that will surely intensify with the population possibly burgeoning toward 11 billion and more. Yes, even as I write, bubonic plague threatens to spread across the world from where it has gripped portions of Sub-Sahara Africa. As we have seen, this region of the world is projected to be overwhelmed with 4 billion people by 2100, many of whom have always been illiterate, had limited access to clean water, and subject to deadly epidemics.

Melinda Gates addressed what might be the principal cause of these issues at a TED presentation in Germany. "Here in Germany, the proportion of people who use contraception is about 66 percent. That's about what you'd expect. In El Salvador, very similar, 66 percent. Thailand, 64 percent.

"But let's compare that to other places like Uttar Pradesh, one of the largest states in India. In fact, if Uttar Pradesh were its own country, it would be the fifth-largest country in the world. Their contraception rate—29 percent. Nigeria, the most populous country in Africa, 10 percent. Chad, 2 percent.

"Let's just take one country in Africa, Senegal. Their rate is about 12 percent. But why is it so low? One reason is that the most popular contraceptives are rarely available. Women in Africa will tell you over and over again that what they prefer today is an injectable. They get it in their arm, and they go [to the doctor] about four times a year—they have to get it every three months—to get their injection. The reason women like it so much in Africa is that they can hide it from their husbands, who sometimes want a lot of children.

"The problem is every other time a woman goes to a clinic in Senegal, that injection is stocked out. It's stocked out 150 days out of the year. So, you can imagine the situation. She walks all this way to get her injection. She leaves her field, sometimes leaves her children, and it's not there. And she doesn't know when it's going to be available again. This is the story across the continent of Africa today."

Distinguished demographer John Bongaarts comments about the same issue: ". . . in most of Africa, family planning programs have been neglected . . ." He continues, "The rationale for these programs lies in the substantial unsatisfied demand for contraception in Sub-Saharan Africa and throughout the developing world. When interviewed about their reproductive preferences, large proportions of women report that they do not want to become pregnant. Some of these women want no more children because they have already achieved their desired family size, while others want to wait before having the next pregnancy.

"Yet a large proportion of these women (more than one-half in some countries) are not practicing effective contraception and are therefore at risk of pregnancy. As a result, unintended pregnancies are common. According to the Guttmacher Institute, more than one-third of pregnancies are unintended in Sub-Saharan Africa."[37]

But should women alone bear responsibility for birth control? I feel there is a better way that may be widely accepted in the twenty-second century. It may help all of humankind, especially the poorest people who are heavily laden with the yoke of ignorance, exploding into domestic violence and crime within their neighborhoods. It may help free them from grinding economic oppression, a black hole wherein metaphysical gravity seems to crush every possible hope of escape. It might free them from debilitating diseases that cause misery and, as we shall see, possibly war.

And, it could be *the second coming* of Earth's flora and fauna.

Here's an example that may help to understand the almost unfathomable humanitarian crisis unfolding in Sub-Sahara Africa that Melinda Gates and John Bongaarts have discussed above. Let's say we begin with the number three (3) and apply the number five (5) to it and to the subsequent results three (3) times. In an *arithmetical* sequence, it looks like this 3, 8, 13, 18. But should we

---

[37] Bongaarts, John, "Africa's challenging demographic future" (Seattle: Humanosphere, 2015)

apply the identical numbers in a *geometric* sequence, we have 3, 15, 75, 375. Now, our food production grows arithmetically, yet our population grows geometrically. As we can see quite clearly, the two numeric sequences are traveling along dramatically different vectors and, at some point, will become irreconcilable.

Therefore, is it numerically feasible that the leaders of Sub-Sahara Africa can quadruple their crop-bearing fields and importation of food to feed the 4 billion people who are projected to live there by 2100? In addition to food, they will need four more of everything over an 80-year period: water infrastructures, sanitation facilities, power stations, electrical grids, dams, hospitals, clinics, schools, universities, roads, bridges, and more. These must be built and rebuilt as they become obsolete or in disrepair over eight decades.

But perhaps they will more accurately need almost five, rather than four, of everything since the basic needs of society are frequently absent there today. Will they call upon other nations to provide the expertise and money for this goliath undertaking, the scope of which is preposterous? I wonder if all the wealth of the world combined could financially underwrite such an enterprise. Indeed, Sub-Sahara Africa's projected population of 4 billion is likened to an entire world, for in 1974, the world's total population was, in fact, 4 billion.

Will the absence of clean water, which has been profoundly and historically lacking, cause more disease, plague, malnutrition, and permanent physical and mental damage to this vast throng of ill-fated people? Will the competing quest for essential needs widen the dozens of perpetual wars that have waged there for decades?

What is more, with Sub-Sahara's present population of 1 billion, human encroachment upon wildlife habitat is endemic and especially problematic in elephant ranges. Therefore, the loss of virtually all megafauna is assured with the presence of 4 billion people, many of whom eat bushmeat. So, we see that the detonation of Africa's population time bomb could be a catastrophe towering above all others in history, its explosion possibly being felt around the globe, dragging untold human lives to mass graves.

Have the leaders of Sub-Sahara Africa devised a plan to address this continental catastrophe, which will inevitably become global? Has a single world leader anticipated this demographic Armageddon with a corresponding strategy to stop it?

Should such a policy exist, it is, apparently, not working, which is why this plan is laid before you now. So, let us proceed with thoughtwork about a proposal to overcome this monumental challenge.

First, it may be helpful to discuss what the plan is *not* before describing what it *is*. This may be necessary since we are examining population management and, therefore, dear reader, others may incorrectly presume the plan involves eugenics. Such an errant notion often derives from labeling general and vague ideas with ill-defined words and instantly creating stereotypical biases based upon that misunderstanding. Consequently, we will consult *Merriam-Webster's Dictionary* for an unambiguous definition of eugenics: "the practice or advocacy of controlled selective breeding of human populations (as by sterilization) to improve the population's genetic composition."

As we shall see quite clearly, this proposal has nothing whatsoever to do with "selective breeding." It does not "improve the population's genetic composition." Indeed, this plan is thoroughly unrelated to genetics, nor does it suggest "sterilization."

Moreover, eugenics carries the connotation of being imposed upon a hapless people—the weakest and most vulnerable of society. Such a notion is cruel and repugnant, for the well-being of these people is, in no small degree, our responsibility. Indeed, all who participate in this proposition do so voluntarily, of their own freewill. What is more, eugenics involves breeding based upon race, whereas those who participate in this program may choose whomsoever they wish as partners in parenting. These freedoms are the oxygen inherent within this arrangement, without which it would instantly suffocate.

With these thoughts in mind, let's continue our discussion of birth control with a description of a new method, possibly a better one, that may look something like the following summarization. Please be mindful, however, that this briefing scarcely touches upon the subject with a cursory review, which is appropriate presently; of course, significant research must be conducted, followed by in-depth feasibility studies, focus study groups, and, eventually, a single implementation test before the final plan.

The proposed plan:

Irrespective of one's genetics, heritage, intelligence, race, religion, social status, strength or weakness, handsomeness or lack thereof, every law-abiding, disease-free, and addiction-free male who reaches the locally recognized appropriate age will receive individual counseling about a family planning program. At least one legal guardian, preferably both of the boy's parents, will be present during this meeting. Of course, parental consent is unnecessary for young men of legal age.

Meaningful career and financial incentives for participating in the program shall be formally presented and discussed; these might include free tuition at a local institute of higher learning, hiring and promotion preferences, and tax reductions. After the meeting, at least one week of consideration must be given by the boy and, if appropriate, his family before reaching a final decision.

Should the young man decide of his own free will to participate in the plan, arrangements will be made to preserve his semen specimens. These will be tested for quantity, shape, and movement, at which time viable samples will be separated into laboratory tubes for freezing. Cryoprotectant agents will be used to safeguard and preserve the sperm cells, which will be stored throughout the life of the young man. The vials will be vouchsafed by registering his handprints upon each one individually, archived by block-chain technology, and cryopreserved at a regional repository. This is a safe, effective method. For example, after a comparative analysis of frozen and fresh sperm samples, four physicians from the University of Illinois and one from Stanford University stated, "Our overall meta-analysis demonstrated no significant difference between the uses of fresh versus cryopreserved testicular sperm for fertilization rates." [38]

After securing a sufficient number of samples, the young man will, by his own volition, receive a vasectomy.

---

[38] Ohlander, Samuel, M.D., Hotaling, James, M.D., M.S., Kirshenbaum, Eric, M.D., Niederberger, Craig M.D., F.A.C.S., Eisenberg, Michael L., M.D. *Impact of fresh versus cryopreserved testicular sperm upon intracytoplasmic sperm injection pregnancy outcomes in men with azoospermia due to spermatogenic dysfunction: a meta-analysis* (Birmingham: American Society for Reproductive Medicine, 2014) Fertility and Sterility Vol. 101, No. 2. 2014.

This painless, non-scalpel procedure can be performed in minutes; both laser and high-intensity ultrasound techniques exist presently, and their perfection is anticipated.

After twenty years, on the condition that he has no criminal record, has contributed significantly to the betterment of society, is mentally sound, and free of disease or addictions, the deposited sperm will be available to the man and his wife for *in vitro fertilization.* Studies compiled by the American Society for Reproductive Medicine suggest a live birth rate of approximately 54.5% for women under 35 when using this method.[39] A regimen of fertility supplements will be available if his wife wishes to use them.

Furthermore, the vasectomy will be reversed upon the man's request by *vasovasostomy* or, if necessary, the more complicated *vasoepididymostomy.* The participant, however, must realize that while reversal technology is advancing, success based on healthy childbirth includes several factors and varies widely.[40] [41] Moreover, some de-

---

[39] "2016 Clinical Summary Report," (Birmingham: American Society for Reproductive Medicine, 2016)

[40] "Vasectomy reversal," (Rochester: Mayo Clinic, 2019)

[41] van Gogen, J., Tekle, F. B., van Roijen, J.H., "Pregnancy rate after vasectomy reversal in a contemporary series: influence of smoking, semen quality and post-surgical use of assisted reproductive techniques," (London: British Journal of Urology, 2012)

gradation of sperm might occur with aging.[42] It may be wise, therefore, to rely solely on cryopreservation.

This plan shall *never* be enforced by laws or regulations, but encouraged by public opinion so as members of a community see its many economic, social, ecological, and peaceful benefits, participants will be drawn to it of their own free will. It hardly needs mentioning, since it is implicitly understood from the benevolent nature of this program, that participants are free to marry whomsoever they wish.

I refer to this as *merit-based parenting*. Now, let us attempt to place this solution in perspective by posing four questions: Has the global human population ever decreased or assumed zero population growth of its own accord? Should we expect it to do so mystically in the future? Is it ethical or responsible to allow the population to possibly exceed 11 billion souls by the year 2100, with a high estimate of 16 billion? Isn't it, therefore, axiomatic that we must adopt and implement a compassionate, benevolent plan to cause its numeric descent?

For if we do not employ a suitable solution, our

---

[42] Harris, Isiah D., MD, Fronczak, Carolyn, Roth, Lauren, MD, Meacham, Randal B., MD, *Fertility and the Ageing Male,* (Bethesda: US National Library of Medicine, 2011)

grandchildren may compete against 11 billion others, or many more, to extract sustenance from an overtaxed Earth, a dynamic that shall increase the incidence of war, famine, disease, and slavery. Merit-based parenting may halt this ongoing catastrophe and, as a martial artist uses the energy of one's opponent to reverse deadly aggression, turn the demise of Earth into an unprecedented rebirth of the flora and fauna, including its human genre.

Now, before others cast a supercilious countenance of contempt upon this solution, I invite them to kindly provide their own and better response to the existential threat facing humanity that looms ever so near. I and all thinkers shall gratefully listen with the most genuine and keen attentiveness. It may, however, be challenging to create another plan that is superior to its simplicity and ease of use. For rather than a woman seeking birth control assistance over approximately thirty years of her life, one or two outpatient surgeries are performed on a man. Indeed, merit-based parenting lifts the exclusive responsibility for birth control from women and its associated complications, such as:

- Health risks for women
- An added expense for the few who can afford it
- Unaffordability for most women
- Regular doctor visits that require time

- Undependability
- Inconsistent use
- Lack of use
- Unavailability

Of course, various birth control methods have been integral to our health systems for many years, but some people might be surprised to know that eugenics is also part of that system. For instance, a blood test that is a prerequisite to marriage prevents the spread of genetic and transmissible diseases such as thalassemia, hemophilia, and sickle cell anemia. Infectious diseases such as syphilis, gonorrhea, and HIV are detected with pre-marriage tests as well. In these cases, engaged couples are forbidden by law from marrying one another or having children together. These are typical examples of *negative eugenics,* used to prevent diseases and the birth of children with permanent mental and physical malformations.

In the future, however, it appears the direction of new branches of medicine may portend the use of genetic modification to produce children who are taller, more beautiful, physically stronger, with IQs that are, for instance, thirty percent higher than average, and even possess an increased chance of a fulfilled and happy life. This is *positive eugenics*. It seems that well-meaning parents may be reluctant not to bestow these blessings upon their posterity. For how could they bear to be confronted by their child, who demands through tears of anger to know why they were not given these superior traits? When unable to compete or possibly even socialize with their genetic superiors, what would be the parent's reason or, more precisely, their excuse? Could such an explanation be supported logically?

And so, the ancient countryside with villages of families scattered here and there seems ever dearer to me as I write these words, and I dream of retreating to this idyllic pastoral life with its beautified simplicity. Oh, to be a free and peasant farmer with a loving peasant wife! The plowing of fields with a team of oxen, the planting, the harvesting—to breathe deeply the aroma of fresh loamy soil. And as my forefathers have done for untold ages, bear our children within this divine realm—the rain and sunlight upon their uplifted faces. Their senses harkened upon the morn, vouchsafed by starry night, with nary a sound, nor sight, nor touch, lest it came from these gentle musings.

If, by chance, I reared a family within this rustic setting, would we eventually receive expressions of piteousness from our taller, more beautiful, brighter, and happier beneficiaries of genetic science? Over a few generations, would the difference between them and us approach that of the Neanderthals and the first humans? Should we choose thus to be left behind? I suppose the social implications could fill a library of books, and I wish we needn't confront them. Yet, it appears that we must. Perhaps an acid test would be this: could recipients of genetic surgery create music that exceeds the artistic mastery of Bach, Brahms, and Beethoven, the insight of Aristotle, the sheer courage and character of King Alfred the Great? Could eugenics bestow kindliness, fairmindedness, healthy psychological boundaries, and the conscientious desire to be a good neighbor? It is unlikely. Alas, we shall see. Even though I wish it were not so, positive eugenics will almost certainly be part of our future. Yet it could be disastrous.

And so, I want to say this with the appropriate emphasis: humanity does not need positive eugenics, but with the most desperate agonies, it cries out for *good parenting.*

If every baby were lovingly held close to the breasts of nurturing, well-adjusted parents for the first two months of their new lives, how would society change? If, during the first sixty days of these little newborns, parents acknowledged the open gaze of baby's eyes with smiles of kindness—every reach of tiny hands touched with the most tender caress—every cry of fear calmed with loving assurance, what societal transformation would we behold? Perhaps all prisons would close in three generations, wars would cease, and we would become good stewards of Earth. Eugenics can never achieve this.

Yet within merit-based parenting's richer society, well-parented young men and women may more readily choose to think noble thoughts, which become noble deeds, culminating in a virtuous life. To be sure, they will be, from their earliest youth, encouraged to entertain such exalted, heroic ideas, flinging wide the door upon its hinges unto the brightness of a thousand generations asking to be born. These shall be the parents of the twenty-second century.

They may enjoy freedoms unknown to us. For example, within social dynamics are immutable numerical laws: as human populations increase, freewill decreases; inversely, as human quantity lessens, freewill abounds. This is obviously territorial. But it is also because a larger populace requires more laws, each of which chips away at individual freedom.

Furthermore, merit-based parenting stands in bright, accented contrast to sterilization, the abandonment of the malformed, or even the widely accepted use of eugenics through prescribed medicine or contraceptives. Such examples of negative birth control become obsolete under the auspices of merit-based parenting, for they will be rarely needed and less seldom, indeed if ever, *wanted*. To be sure, merit-based parenting attaches a higher value to human life, birth under its influence being a *herald-worthy event, a celebratory event* throughout a neighborhood and community. Whereas, the numerical effect of the United Nations' projected possibility of over 11 billion souls tends to devalue humanity, a new member of this unimaginably vast throng being rather uneventful and unnoticed by others besides the parents, for whom it is often seen as a burden. Indeed, many times the birth of a child is met with disdain.

I recall particular disregard for baby girls when traveling in India, for there girls are often considered a heavy liability compared to a boy who can more helpfully earn the family's daily bread.

The train from India to Nepal on which I was a passenger stopped for only five minutes at a small rustic town, not much larger than a village. Being filled with wanderlust, I was quick to disembark even for that short amount of time for a brief look at the market, which had been arranged at the turnstile. All too soon, the whistle blew, and I raced alongside the moving train, bearing down in a dead run, and, grabbing a railing, swung aboard. Satisfied with a feeling of sporting victory, I plopped into my seat.

It was then, dear friends, that I saw a sight I shall never forget, although its light met my eyes for no more than five seconds and then was gone. A lovely girl with jet black hair and a complexion almost as dark was rushing toward the train. She apparently had spent considerable time adorning her raven locks, cut in a pageboy style, pulled back from her pretty face with a blue ribbon. The ribbon matched her blue polka-dot dress, which was carefully ironed and pressed. I see, even now, the flashing consternation that affected her exquisitely feminine facial features as she hurried toward the passing train, realizing she was too late. She tried so desperately to be on time.

She watched the train rush away from her.

For, you see, I was told her parents had broken her legs when she was a baby so that she could be a useful beggar, her legs ever since being in a permanent akimbo position. Thus, she lifted herself with both hands, hurriedly swinging her body forward, again and again, to catch the train to beg of its passengers. Would her inhuman parents, who broke the legs of their very own baby, not viciously beat her for bringing home an empty beggar's cup? Such an arduously long, such an interminably long and rigorously pain-filled life she has suffered, locked within the inescapable prison of her body under the implacable wardenship of those taskmasters to whom she cries out with innocent travesty the words *father, mother!*

Thus, the tenderness with which she dwells in my heart grows through the years. Although I did not meet her, I christened her Nidhi, an Indian name for girls meaning *my treasure,* and it is to her among all people upon the Earth that I have dedicated this book.

Oh, precious Nidhi! When you find sleep, do you dream that you are a ballerina dancing on stage with delicate grace and charm amidst the soft pastels of a Degas painting? Do you dream of waltzing with a prince in a ballroom in which you are the loveliest maiden of all? Do you find yourself running with abandon through a flowered meadow?

Then the terrifying awakening!

If I had disembarked at the next station and taken another train back to the village where I saw you, could I have found you? Without the ability to understand English, could you have known of my desire to help you? Could I have done anything?

My dear Nidhi represents the atrocious misery of millions upon millions of similar innocent lives that shall never be endured 'neath the heel of reckless, cruel parents when merit-based parenting is the norm.

Now, we leave this sacred moment to continue our discussion, but, my treasure, you shall always be with me.

Not only might merit-based parenting resolve the calamitous population threat, but also conceivably propel the poorer nations in an upward spiral toward a zenith unparalleled in all their historical achievements. Within a few generations, poverty may significantly lessen, for *poverty causes population growth,* and *population growth causes poverty.* 'Tis neither one nor the other that is the culprit, but both. The United Nations Population Fund (UNPF) provides insight into that subtle economic nuance.

"If adolescent girls in Brazil and India were able to

wait until their early twenties to have children, the increased economic productivity would equal more than \$3.5 billion and \$7.7 billion, respectively." In other words, rather than a non-working mother with one or more babies, all of whom are financial liabilities, there would be one working adolescent girl who is an economic asset, and this more favorable situation would be multiplied millions of times over. The common worker would be the greatest benefactor.

The UNPF continues, "Developing countries with large youth populations and declining fertility rates could see their economies soar, provided they invest heavily in young people's education and health and protect their rights, according to *The State of World Population 2014*. Potential economic gains could be realized through a 'demographic dividend,' which can occur when a country's working-age population grows larger relative to dependent populations, the report shows."

Of course, a latent effect of population reduction could involve declining markets of scale wherein there are fewer consumers to buy products and services. Thus, an economic equilibrium must be targeted with careful planning and forethought for the near and distant future, so trends can be anticipated several decades in advance.

Another betterment of the merit-based parenting system of population management is the decrease in air pollution, water pollution, and food pollution, which will doubtlessly improve human health. Merit-based parenting will also lessen human encroachment upon the flora and fauna ushering in their restoration. Overall, quality will replace quantity.

And of course, merit-based parenting's self-chosen men, who have successfully distinguished themselves from among others, will select the finest women—those who are not merely attractive but also of the highest moral character measured against the background of a benevolent, functional society in which the family is highly esteemed. The competition of men to earn the right to reproduce, the competition amongst women to give birth, both competing to have a family shall lift us ever upward and upward. Thus, the family might be *more cherished than ever before in human history.*

I predict this elegant wooing of the finest men seeking the finest women may be played out on the stage of *courting* rather than dating. This, I feel, will occur as a natural result of merit-based parenting. In other words, I predict the adoption of courting as a norm will be an organic evolution rather than one that is imposed, which is a freedom thematic to all social advancements suggested in this book.

Indeed, as in what may have been more civilized times, when men would call upon a young lady in her parlor with both her parents present and, perhaps, have light conversation over tea, courting may become culture and custom of our future societies. If the man calls again or is reinvited for tea, the suitor may join the family dinner, for example, as the two potential marriage partners become better acquainted. During these visits, the man and his future mother and father-in-law would also learn more about one another. After some time courting in this way, followed by the announcement of an engagement, the two paramours may spend time at concerts, the theater, picnics at the beach, dinner at restaurants or walks in the local park, for instance.

These are neither rules nor laws, mind you. I foresee them becoming accepted norms simply through the influence of merit-based parenting but, of course, never forced. At the same time, courting may lead to happier, more successful marriages. By contrast, dating typically engenders premarital indiscrimination, which statistically decreases the likelihood of good, long-lasting marriages. After all, I think we will see that courting accompanied those societies that were composed of the happiest individual members and families.

So dear friends, we might give some thought to the virtues of courting. For without the gentility and high morals embodying the idea and indeed the art of courtship, I feel quite certain that we shall never ascend the glorious summit to which we are divinely called.

Moreover, I feel that upon closer and more open-minded consideration of merit-based parenting, and possibly courtship, we may find that both men and women will be extremely motivated to excel, to maintain a healthy body, mind, and soul, flourishing unabated atop the absolute pinnacle of healthy competition.

This unshackling of the competent is, however, a revolutionary act before the taskmasters of serfdom. For competency is their bitterest enemy, exposing the errors of their ways. Therefore, it is they, above all, who will abhor our emancipation. So, we, dear friends, must assume leadership over these usurpers of the nations, yet with fair-mindedness, even to them. But let them know this oceanic change has begun and is coming in interminable waves that no ideological seawall can resist.

So, I challenge the thinkers who are among us to fine-tune the introduction and implementation of this social giant stride and, in so doing, hasten its practice. It would, however, be quite impossible to present a detailed plan here. For such an all-encompassing plan must be created among several great minds, working closely together. When at last their master plan is completed, it will not remain static but shall ever change, just as the plan of battle changes instantly after the first shot is fired.

Indeed, such a plan must go through the process of being implemented and crafted, then implemented and crafted again, and so on, as various strengths, weaknesses, threats, and opportunities present themselves. Nevertheless, as we have before mentioned, the successful results of these thoughtworks will most assuredly involve the change of popular opinion of the masses. Yes, the key that unlocks this futuristic door is influencing popular opinion, so the masses *want* the proposed plan of merit-based parenting with its increased prosperity, cleaner, safer cities, better families and home life, with more and far higher achievements further benefiting their respective societies.

By sharp contrast to instilling the benevolent desire for these benefits is governmental enforcement, which I neither envision nor recommend and would be *anathema* to the future I foresee. Indeed, for merit-based parenting to work, the majority of a nation must willingly welcome it simply because it improves their lives.

For example, a remarkable improvement will occur as a by-product of merit-based parenting in regions that practice *consanguinity*. This is the marriage of first cousins, aunts and nephews, uncles and nieces, brothers and sisters, and other incestuous relationships. Such consanguineous relationships dramatically increase the incidence of irreversible congenital mental disabilities. Merit-based parenting could significantly reduce the occurrence of these malformations, which is why I posed this question in the foreword: Is it realistic to think that war, the accomplice of ecological recklessness, is not inevitable?

And here I will further ask, is it possible for the seething hotbed of Arabia and the Middle East to cool and a blessed, long-lasting peace to reign in its place, war being a forgotten barbarism? For I feel that consanguinity and its complement of mental impairment are responsible for the incessant wars that plague that region. Peace diplomacy is virtuous, even heroic in some cases, yet I wonder if this is woefully superficial given the following facts.

In the *New York Times,* Sarah Kernshaw wrote, "Across the Arab world today an average of 45 percent of married couples are related, according to Dr. Nadia Sakati, a pediatrician and senior consultant for the genetics research center at [the] King Faisal Specialist Hospital in Riyadh. In some parts of Saudi Arabia, particularly in the south . . . the rate of marriage among blood relatives ranges from 55 to 70 percent, among the highest rates in the world, according to the Saudi government."[43]

Consanguinity in Asia and Africa, for example, is possibly as frequent, or more so, as in Arabia yet without the supporting statistics that are more readily available from Arabic nations. In his work, *Inbreeding in Humans,* Eugene Ochap says, "In fact, in many large populations of Asia and Africa, twenty to fifty percent of all unions are that of consanguineous marriages."

It appears that the Asian country of Pakistan also has an old tradition of consanguinity. "Professor Steve Jones,

---

[43] Kernshaw, Sarah, "Saudi Arabia Awakes to the Perils of Inbreeding," (New York: *New York Times,* 2003)

from University College London, said the common practice in [Pakistan] communities for cousins to marry each other increased the risk of birth defects. Studies have shown that 55 percent of British Pakistanis are married to first cousins–and in Bradford [England], this rises to 75 percent."[44]

In another report, "Consanguinity is common in North Africa, and the estimates range from 40 to 49% of all marriages in Tunisia and 29–33% in Morocco. Consequently, recessive disorders are common in the North Africa region, and we give some examples. Thalassaemia and sickle cell disease/anemia constitute the most common inherited recessive disorders globally and they are common in North Africa, but with immigration they have spread to Europe and to other parts of the world. Another example is *familial Mediterranean fever*, which is common in the Eastern Mediterranean area."[45]

So, it seems that the peacemakers of Arabia, the Middle East, Africa, and Asia would, therefore, enthusiastically welcome merit-based parenting.

It is our misfortune that such a change requires much time. Yet, it is our *fortune* that we, who create change, are

____

[44] Kelly, Tom, "Bradford is very inbred," (London, *Daily Mail, 2011)*
[45] Anwar, Wagida A., Khyatti, Meriem and Hemmenki, Kari "Consanguinity and genetic diseases in North Africa and immigrants to Europe," (Oxford: European Journal of Public Health, 2014)

masters of creative thinking, and so, we have the advantage in evolving social norms and mores. Therefore, I invoke this timely challenge to all: Think, dear friends, and redeem yourself!

Finally, those who realize the unique implications of humans upon humanity may also realize the virtue of the most well-adjusted of society being parents to human babies, within whom are powers both diabolical and divine. May merit-based parenting be the germinating rich loamy soil, the pure water, and lifegiving sunlight of the latter.

Should these three elements, symbolizing nurturing parenthood, be absent in the life of a newborn, the child's unconscious mind will develop improperly. Then, with its mental powers virtually supreme among all things terrestrial, lay waste to fields, forests, mountains, rivers, streams, oceans, and all life within them. Hasn't history proven this?

So, we see that the care of this new human mind, this vast super engine of unlimited authority with its endless reservoir of creativity, should be given superb care lest humanity arbitrarily parent more ecological warmongers and robber barons.

For we all agree that powerful weapons must be overseen with designated care, and that the most powerful of these must be given determinate attention of the most extraordinary levels.

Therefore, should not the minds that will control them

be given even a keener guardianship? And this not within cold stainless-steel laboratories wherein unsmiling scientists amble hither and yon in white smocks, grasping clipboards. Let it be in the stable, peaceable, loving home of a well-adjusted mother and father.

Now, we will recapitulate this chapter by expressing it in one algebraic equation:

$$popular\ opinion +$$
$$plant\text{-}based\ diet + Earthly\ cities\ and\ transportation +$$
$$merit\text{-}based\ parenting = Earthly\ balance$$

or

$$\{po + pbd + Ect + mbp\} = Eb$$

Thus, we are divinely summoned to return to the Garden. In the meantime, we can, and should, implement micro-solutions that will help. But—let us put away false talk—they will never stop the locomotive avalanche of ecological perils that barrel down upon us. Only macro solution $\{po + pbd + Ect + mbp\}$ shall accomplish this and without variation.

In other words, $\{po + pbd + Ect\} \neq Eb$ because without merit-based parenting (mbp) the population imbalance would overwhelm and defeat the other subsets. And clearly, {mbp + pbd + Ect} ≠ Eb since acceptance and implementation of these three subsets would be impossible without popular opinion (po). Neither does {po + mbp + Ect} = Eb as this would retain ecological imbalance, pollution, epidemic human disease, and the miserable deaths of 56 billion animals each year should we subtract plant-based diet (pbd) from the equation.

And, {po + mbp + pbd} ≠ Eb for subtracting Earthly cities and transportation (Ect) retains our agreement with the giant ogre who kills over 1 million of us year after year, more than 5 billion fauna annually, and utterly destroys millions of acres of flora each year while polluting the air we breathe. It also retains the corpse-gray cities, which are anathema before nature.

We will not discuss the remaining twelve combinations of subsets, neither of which will achieve Eb. Therefore, only {po + pbd + Ect + mbp} and Eb are equals. Indeed, Eb exclusively = {po + pbd + Ect + mbp}, there being no other formulaic path to Eb. So, when we speak of {Eb}, {po + pbd + Ect + mbp} is precisely what we are expressing.

Also, {po → pbd → Ect → mbp} → Eb indicating its sequential hierarchy. For the most vigorous nature of the equation lies within this critical path. Ideally, each subset should be switched on before the proceeding subset in nonnegotiable sequence. Its initial viability and continued sustainability may depend upon this for two primary reasons: first, pbd and Ect are becoming norms in larger sections of society, and this acceptability is a base upon which we can build. Secondly, the wider acceptance of pbd and Ect will, in turn, raise conscious human awareness, which is a vital prerequisite to the acceptance of the last and integral subset of mbp.

The equation will later, however, succeed its sequential nature, becoming bidirectional as its variables empower one another, eventually becoming one pulsating unit, a set of new, dynamic social mores. Initially, however, public opinion {po}, plant-based diet {pbd}, and Earthly cities and transportation {Ect} are preconditions of the remaining subset of the mathematical statement, which of course, is merit-based parenting {mbp}.

And, population management achieved by merit-based parenting {mbp} is firmly integral to Earthly balance, and this without omission or replacement. *Any* plan to halt and, moreover, reverse ecological collapse that omits the element of {mbp} imperils precious thoughtwork by absorbing essential energy needed to materially arrive at the solution corresponding to the right side of the equation.

Chapter Three

Ten Things You Can Do In the Next Twenty-Four Hours

HAPPY holidays! shouted a friend across the cordial brouhaha of last-minute shoppers, cheery faces one and all, picking up their gourmet fare for the big dinner. Many held packages gaily wrapped, and here and there, little groups of friends who had met serendipitously shared laughter. The big coats, stocking caps, gloved hands, and ear-muffed ears added an unmistakable snug and safe feeling. And with Scrooges' nephew Freddy I say, "God bless it!"

Amidst this respite from the long labors and woes of the year, we feel all is right with the world. And while this sprightly celebration of good cheer is a right thing—a needed thing—we mustn't be lulled into thinking the eco-logical crisis will resolve itself.

The first 212 days of this year, up until August 1, 2018, humanity has devoured one year's worth of food, water, carbon, land, and timber. To maintain this voracious consumption, as we have seen, we would need the equivalent of 1.7 Earths. With this rapacious treatment of the majestically beautiful and abundant home that our most gracious lord has freely and generously bestowed upon us—even the murder of his royal messengers, the flora and fauna—come war, famine, plague, and slavery. These shall not stop at the walls of our great cities. A loaf of bread shall buy a bag of gold. The mighty militaries cannot guard us nor fight without food and water, so even these shall disperse into roaming packs of scavengers. No one, no one whomsoever shall escape the apocalypse.

To turn away this behemoth of horror rushing at incomprehensible speed upon us, as we have seen, we must begin at the only beginning: *our bodies.* For those who care for their bodies will most likely redeem the Earth, since typically, it is they who will, in turn, actively care for the flora and fauna. By dramatic contrast, those who love an unhealthy diet more than their bodies, will probably continue eating unhealthily, the invisibility of the flora and fauna's divinity prevailing upon them.

Dear friends, is this not blasphemous? Be different

than this.

Be heroic.

For, amongst the long and winding cavalcade of history, now is the most urgent time for heroes and heroines to step forward. Therefore, think and act healthily for such a mentality and behavior is prerequisite to all else in this book, especially $\{po + pbd + Ect + mbp\} = Eb$.

In addition to protecting our health, there are many everyday deeds we must perform. While these micro-deeds will not ultimately save us, let us place them in their proper priority with this supposition:

Imagine you are a citizen of a city-state that is besieged by a myriad of enemies, vastly outnumbering your people. Amidst the thunder of the advancing army, your leader rallies the citizens to reinforce the city walls. Pointing to ten thousand sandbags, he shouts, "You, there! You and the others build a blockade with those bags against the city gates! This will hold the invaders until we can regroup!" Would you say, "It's no use," and walk away? Or would you fight, although victory is but a flickering candle in a storm? If you would not fight, you are not and never will be one of us.

As the leader of the city-state knew that precious time was running out for them to regroup, likewise, precious time is running out for us to regroup should we hope to overcome the immense challenge set before us. In the meantime, we must all pull together to stem the approaching tide. While {po + pbd + Ect + mbp} = Eb must be our vision that we work toward, it can only be achieved with long-term planning. In the meantime, these are some, *but clearly not all,* of the things we can do to save the flora and fauna, all of which you can easily begin within the next twenty-four hours:

1. First and foremost, try a plant-based diet. Nothing helps your health and the Earth more than this. So, let's look at a delicious and easy-to-prepare plant-based menu for one day:

<u>Breakfast</u>
Eco Smoothie
Using all organic ingredients, place the following items in a blender: a frozen banana, spinach or kale, celery, blueberries, strawberries. Add 12 oz of filtered water. Blend. While blending, add one scoop of green pea protein powder sweetened with stevia. Drink and enjoy this extremely healthy smoothie.

Molasses Oatmeal with almonds, walnuts, and cinnamon
After your smoothie, enjoy a bowl of organic oat-

meal. You may want to add four or five organic almonds, four of five organic walnut halves (more may cause weight gain), a tablespoon of organic molasses topped with a generous sprinkling of organic cinnamon.

This is a carbohydrate-rich meal that will boost your energy all day long. The almonds and walnuts provide the healthy fat and protein your body loves; the molasses is rich in iron for stamina; the cinnamon is an antifungal. And the oatmeal is one of the healthiest foods we can eat. Altogether, it tastes marvelous.

<u>Lunch</u>
Avocado Salad
Using all organic ingredients, peel and slice an avocado, mix with baby leaf spinach, cherry tomatoes, slices of red onion, shredded carrots, chopped celery, sliced red bell pepper. Sprinkle with olive oil and apple cider vinegar.

Enjoy with an organic apple or an organic orange along with a glass of organic carrot juice, organic apple juice or another healthy organic juice *not* from concentrate.

<u>Dinner</u>
Here are three delectable dinner choices, all of which are my recipes that I enjoy at home:

Pasta Fusilli Rossellini
Using all organic ingredients, prepare gluten-free pasta fusilli, mixed with tomato paste, olive oil, fresh basil leaves, fresh spinach leaves, black o-lives, and red onion slices. The amount of each in-gredient is up to you.
Enjoy with a glass of organic grape juice, *not* from concentrate, in a beautiful wine glass. *Salute!*

Enchilada Champs Elysees
Two organic vegan enchiladas on a bed of organic Champs Elysees salad (green leaf lettuce, frisee, radicchio, and carrots). Sometimes you can find the organic vegan enchiladas readymade and the organic Champs Elysees salad ready-mixed at the local market.

Taste of Old Kashmir
Organic brown rice mixed with Kashmiri curry, organic green peas, organic peanuts, organic baby spinach leaves, all topped with organic coconut flakes. Positively delicious!

<u>Dessert</u>
Here are two original ideas I created for dessert:

Queen of the May Parfait
Pour 4 tbsps. of molasses in a dessert cup or water goblet. Add one scoop of chocolate vegan protein powder (sweetened with stevia, not sugar). Over this, add 7 oz. of sweet potato puree and top with another swirl or two of molasses, then crown with a red, long-stemmed cherry. Served chilled. With its three layers of different-colored ingredients, visible through the cup or goblet, and its bright red crown, Queen of the May Parfait makes a royal after-dinner presentation.

Sweet Pecan Pie
Bake 4 sweet potatoes and store overnight in the refrigerator. While baking a gluten-free pie crust, peel the sweet potatoes (compost the skins later) and mash with chocolate vegan protein and pecan pieces. Place this in your baked pie crust, add swirls of molasses, and cover with pecan halves. Serve cool. Invite your friends over and enjoy!

2. Try driving less. I live without a car and love it. When needing transportation, which is about twice a month, I rent a car. When renting, the subcompact I select uses gas so efficiently that I am never charged for fuel. Consequently, I have not been to a gas station in a long while and *do not* miss the experience! Neither do I miss car insurance payments, routine maintenance, car washing, concern about car burglaries, selling an old car, buying a new one, and many other car hassles. Of course, I am leaving a much smaller footprint upon the Earth.

According to recent studies by the Environmental Protection Agency, motor vehicles in the United States produce approximately fifty percent of pollutants like volatile organic compounds, nitrogen oxide, and particulate matter. Much of America's carbon monoxide emissions also come from automobiles. In urban areas, harmful automotive emissions are responsible for anywhere between fifty and ninety percent of air pollution. The most damaging of these pollutants may be particulate matter, which is a combination of acids, metals, soil, dust, and organic chemicals. Particulate matter less than ten micrometers in diameter is small enough to enter our lungs, damaging them and our heart, as well. Nitrogen dioxide can have a similar effect.

Yet, motor vehicles create more ecological damage than the poisonous fumes from their exhaust. The factories that manufacture automobiles and the parts for them send poison into the air from the paint, plastic, and rubber products they make. Moreover, cars often leave puddles of antifreeze wherever driven. It is not uncommon for birds, dogs, cats, and other animals to mistake the antifreeze for water and drink it only to die a torturous death. As we have seen, millions of us are killed and injured, and billions of animals are killed by cars year after year.

It is quite possible for some of us to emancipate ourselves from the multiple troubles of a car. Many cities in Europe, because they were designed before the advent of the automobilc, are walking cities. There are fewer in North America, but they exist and are a real joy to live in because, today, it is a wonderful feeling to be liberated from the oppression of a car. So, I believe that all who can live comfortably without a car would be happier by doing so and, of course, leave a much less negative impact upon the flora and fauna. They will save money, too. According to the American Public Transportation Association, families that use public transportation, rather than driving cars, can reduce their household expenses by $6,200 annually.

We may want to try walking more. Rather than getting in the car when you feel restless or the need to get out and about, try going for a walk instead. The fresh air and exercise may give you a new attitude about life. You may become more animated, pleasing, and even entertaining to those around you. If you do this regularly, your health will improve, too, whereas driving probably does none of these things and may cause stress and irritability. Driving costs money, but walking is free.

If you live within a mile or so of your grocery store, it's more fun and gratifying to put a backpack on your shoulders and walk there. I do this about twice a week. When you arrive, you'll feel more alive and appear healthier and friendlier to those you meet. If you have a few minutes, stop and share a cup of tea with a friend. Buy a few items, place them in your backpack, and enjoy the walk home. Should you live in a city designed for cars, rather than humans, walking to the store may not be feasible. In this case, you may want to think about moving to an area that is walking friendly.

Riding a bike may be a fun solution. I can pedal to a specialty health food market that is four miles from my home and arrive as quickly as by driving a car. I enjoy it much more than driving since I bike along a riverside park where trees and birds provide scenic beauty. Of course, riding the bike also boosts endorphins, increases mental alertness, and exercises my circulatory, respiratory, and lymphatic systems.

Packing a picnic lunch for two and riding a bicycle to a park is also more fun than driving because the food and companionship will be more gratifying after the fresh air and exercise. If logistically possible, some of us may be able to ride a bike to work; the physical and mental health benefits could be immeasurable. The Danes know this well. According to several studies, they're considered the happiest people in the world, and I suspect part of this may be due to riding bikes, which they do religiously.

Working remotely may save time, money, and the environment. If you are an employer, eliminating an office and a parking space multiplied by several or many employees who begin working at home could have a significant economic impact on your bottom line. If you are the employee in this instance and work remotely, you will save money by using less gasoline, receive a discount on your car insurance, spend less on car repairs, and save considerable time, as well. Should you have a family with one or more cars, in this arrangement, you may be able to sell one of them, eliminating half of your car expenses, and possibly placing the profits from the sale in the bank.

And rather than driving a car, think like our young lovers of the future, Dane and Ingrid—if it's available, take the underground.

3. Recycle. A compelling reason to recycle is the gargantuan swirling pile of trash between the United States mainland and Hawaii, known as the Great Pacific Garbage Patch. It is presently three times the size of France. This was determined by a study conducted with aerial sensors that reconstructed 3D shapes of the debris, concluding that this blight upon the Earth is 1.6 million km2, weighs 80,000 tons, and contains 1.8 trillion pieces of plastic. This equates to 250 pieces for every human in the world. So, please *never* purchase a plastic drinking bottle. This is where it will likely be sent.

Here is another dramatic example of the need to recycle: according to the Environmental Protection Agency, should an office building of 7,000 workers recycle all its office paper waste for a year, it would be the equivalent of taking almost 400 cars off the road.

To be sure, recycling makes a difference. So, we must recycle all paper. We must recycle glass bottles. As much as possible, we must avoid buying anything in plastic, but should we do so, we must recycle it, too. And rather than using paper or plastic bags when shopping at the grocery store, we must take our own bags that we use repeatedly. We should even recycle by composting.

4. Compost. Banana peels, orange peels, apple cores, avocado skins and seeds, etcetera, etcetera, should be composted. In a year, one person's compost can easily weigh over one hundred pounds, so this is an essential part of recycling.

Place compost items in a bag. To avoid unwanted odor or attraction of insects, it may be a good idea to place the bag in the refrigerator. When it is full, dig a hole and empty the bag there, returning its contents to the

Earth. The soil will be particularly nutritious in your composting area and ready for your garden.

5. Plant a garden. The taste of a homegrown tomato will most likely be an expansion of your taste buds, setting a new standard for the taste of tomatoes as well as most vegetables and fruits you grow yourself. Visit your local nursery or hardware store, where you may find seeds, planting instructions and advice about starting your garden. While there, ask about planting trees, too.

6. Plant trees. As Queen Caroline has so elegantly taught us, trees are a source of wonder and beauty who oxygenate our world while attracting an array of fauna such as birds who bless us with their songs and visual charm. To only begin to appreciate these ideas, imagine for a moment if all the trees were suddenly gone. How would your neighborhoods, parks, schools, businesses, and cities look? How would this make you feel? Besides depression, we also may find it decidedly more difficult to breathe. Indeed, trees provide many benefits, including:

- Increased property value
- Soil retention
- Cooler homes during the summer from shade
- Reduced cooling bill

- Cooler environment
- Protecting streets from Sun deterioration
- Providing a home and protection for birds
- Providing a home and protection for fauna
- Lowering blood pressure
- Calming us unconsciously
- Creating a subtle, unconscious happiness
- Most importantly, they generate oxygen for us and all the other members of the fauna

If you have a yard or other land, visit your local garden nursery and seek their advice about which trees are best suited for your area. You may wish to consider planting a variety of trees, not only for exterior landscaping but also for the various birds who desperately need a home. Both objectives can be met by planting tall trees, medium-sized trees, and smaller trees. This is aesthetically appealing and will attract a wider array of bird species. Adding shrubs to this variation of tree height will also increase the beauty of your property and give the birds a much-needed place to hide from predators, thereby saving their lives and, in turn, attracting even more species.

Remember, within our cities, we have taken almost all the birds' habitat, so we must plant more trees for them to survive.

Should you not own property on which to plant trees,

you may want to learn about the tree canopy of your city. Most cities need more trees, and helping to promote a more fully spread canopy is a good deed all of us should do. Meeting with your city forester is an excellent place to begin; if your city does not have a forester, determine who is responsible for forest husbandry in your city. Meet him or her with the intent of becoming a supportive volunteer.

If no program for trees exists in your city or if an existing organization is not addressing a need to increase the city canopy, consider making this your vision. Several organizations may support you in such a campaign. Contact them and start today.

7. *Feed wild birds*. Please remember, we've lost 3 billion wild birds in the U.S. and Canada since 1970, so they need our help. What is more, feeding them is an awareness experience for us, and consequently, we benefit almost as much as the birds we feed. For the more compassionately we care for the flora and fauna, the more vividly we will see their divine messages.

More birds will come to your feeders and, therefore, survive longer and more easily if we offer filtered water and different types of food placed in the noon and afternoon shade. Placing them in the shade is important because we don't want the water to be too hot to drink but cool and refreshing; nor do we want the feeders to be in the Sun where the birds must endure the pounding heat.

You may wish to plant fruit-bearing trees that provide shade, shelter, and food. Oak, dogwood, mulberry, cherry, apple, and peach trees are excellent food choices. Birds also love purple coneflowers, sunflowers, cardinal flowers, trumpet honeysuckles, Virginia creepers, and elderberries. A well-rounded buffet also includes:

1. purified water
2. hulled sunflower seeds (this leaves no hull-litter)
3. black oil sunflower seeds in the shell
4. safflower
5. peanuts in the shell (must be raw with no salt)
6. suet
7. organic peanut butter
8. organic fruit
9. hummingbird nectar

Hummingbird nectar is easily made from this recipe: Start with 1/4 cup of organic white sugar, mixed until dissolved with 1 cup of filtered water. Please, never use ready-mixed nectar that is dyed red. The feeder must be cleaned, and new nectar added every few days, especially when the temperature exceeds 90 degrees. But it's worth it! Just remember the heroic intercontinental flight of Mercury, and you will be eager to help.

Millet is not suggested since it is unpopular with most

birds; however, it does attract sparrows who kill song-birds, which is one of the leading causes of wild bird deaths. Yet, the leading cause of wild bird death is feral cats, or cats who are allowed to roam outside by their owner. It is estimated that 2.2 million birds are killed by cats each year in the United States alone, year after year. So, please *always* keep your cats inside.

8. Avoid commercial cleaning products. The U.S. Geological Survey reports that water coming out of nine wastewater treatment plants in the Northwest United States contained chemicals from household cleaning products such as fragrances from lotions, shampoos, and antibacterial agents from hand soap, sunscreen chemicals, cosmetics, and a considerable number of pharmaceuticals. Treatment plants are not required to remove this toxicity, and they pour it into our rivers.

The U.S. Environmental Protection Agency has identified personal care products as "emerging contaminants of concern" for fish and other wildlife in our rivers and streams. These chemicals can cause endocrine system disruption in aquatic wildlife, which may further cause a compromised immune system, neurological disorders, reproductive and behavioral maladies, and quite possibly cancer. As other animals consume fish that are poisoned with these chemicals, a biological accumulation occurs, moving up the food chain with increased toxicity. In other words, any animal who eats fish or drinks water contaminated by these chemicals also ingests the chemicals we pour down our drains.

Ironically, "personal cleaning products" do not efficiently clean the human body, nor are "household cleaners" necessary to clean dishes, countertops, the bathroom, or clothing. So, it is profoundly contradictive that most people spend money on these items that are unnecessary and inefficient, contaminating our water and our bodies. For many of these products contain ingredients that are absorbed into the bloodstream within seconds, which, in turn, crash our immune system. For instance, almost all shampoos contain Sodium Lauryl Sulfate or Sodium Laureth Sulfate (SLS), which cause their bubbling, sudsing action. This is nothing less than poison, and attacks the human immune system.

Yet, friction from scrubbing with water removes an equal number of bacteria and with the same efficiency as scrubbing with soap or shampoo. And commercial deodorant, for example, can be replaced with baking soda mixed with a few drops of water. Toothpaste is available at health food stores that is free of the toxins found in conventional toothpaste. Dishes and clothes can be cleaned with hot water and without any detergents at all; and, you can add one-half cup of baking soda to a load of laundry to eliminate odors. Scrubbing a stain on clothing with apple cider vinegar and baking soda, followed by a machine wash *without* any detergent might remove most stains. Apple cider vinegar disinfects and cleans showers, toilets, and countertops. Most sinks and bathtubs can be easily cleaned with nothing more than a wet washcloth, leaving them sparkling white. If we feel the need for an abrasive cleaner for sinks and tubs, baking soda is an abrasive cleaner that never leaves a scratch.

Should ants, wasps, or other insects drop by uninvited, rather than using insecticides to repel them, you might try essential oil of cinnamon. Insecticides are harmful to you, your family, pets, plants, and friendly bugs such as butterflies, ladybugs, and bees, whose work of pollination is integral to the ecosystem. But pure cinnamon cassia oil diluted with water is harmless and effective for managing unwanted insects. Spraying it near doors, for example, where ants may have been invading your home, will repel them while adding a fresh, clean smell to your house. This works well with wasps, too, who might have nested in an area too close for comfort. It won't kill them, but they find cinnamon intolerable and will seek another place to build their homes. Cinnamon oil should repel any insect.

So, let's live in a toxic-free home by avoiding commercial cleaning products and clean instead with water, apple cider vinegar, or baking soda. Let's enjoy cleaner, younger looking skin and hair by bathing in warm water with a little scrubbing. We'll save money. And, we'll help keep our rivers, streams, ponds, lakes, and oceans cleaner.

9. Use less energy. It is a good idea to examine our lives, seeking ways to use less electricity, gas, coal, and any other energy source. Here are only a few thoughts.

Heating and cooling costs constitute nearly half of an average home's utility bills, so the easiest way to save energy at home is to lower our heat in the winter and use less air conditioning in the summer. Turn off the heat or air conditioning during temperate weather and open the windows, welcoming the fresh air. We can also wear a sweater during the day at home when it is cooler and wear pajamas in bed at night with an extra blanket, rather than turning up the heater. Of course, we want to always turn off the heat or air when leaving home, unless we live in a severe clime. We can save 80 percent of the electricity used to light our homes quite simply by using LED light bulbs throughout them. For an LED bulb producing 1100 to 1499 lumens, creates the equivalent of 75 watts, but uses only 6 watts. Moreover, one LED bulb can last eighteen years.

The electricity used by electronics when turned off or in standby mode, known as *phantom loads*, is a significant source of energy drain. It is estimated that 75% of the energy for household electronics is used when they are turned off. So, unplug your electronic devices when asleep or away from home, or use a *smart power strip* that will do this automatically.

Using energy-efficient appliances, heating and air conditioning units, and time-regulated thermostats will help, as will weatherizing your home by installing insulation, sealing doors, windows, and vents, all of which will retain heat in the winter and coolness in the summer. If the weather permits, sun dry clothes. Thaw frozen items overnight as this will require less cooking energy and, during the winter months, leave the oven door open after cooking so the heat will help warm the house.

10. Use less water. When brushing our teeth, turn off the tap. This will save one quart or one liter per minute. Should we brush our teeth for one minute, twice daily, that's an annual savings of about 180 gallons of drinking water. Let's be sure the washer is full before washing clothes. When showering, we use up to four gallons, or seventeen liters, of water each minute, something to be mindful of when bathing. Catching rainwater can save on our water bill when watering our gardens, flowers, lawns, and trees. This is also better than treated tap water. Fix a leaky faucet. Its steady drip may amount to gallons of wasted water every day.

It is sobering to realize that seventy percent of all

freshwater is used to produce our food. Indeed, food requires significant amounts of water to grow and nurture, so wasting food inadvertently wastes water. Therefore, it is wise to eat all the food we prepare by saving uneaten portions for another meal. A plant-based diet, incidentally, will reduce our water footprint by thirty-five percent.

Finally, although the Earth's water tables remain constant, the human population grows exponentially, decreasing the ratio of water per person. This is probably the most compelling reason to use water wisely. For, besides oxygen, it is our most precious possession.

Now, as we put these ten ideas into action, always envision a successful outcome, for we shall win if we pull forward together. *Be certain of it.* Yet, we must work smart, work hard, and work until we win. Each of us must do his or her part implementing these ten ecologically sound deeds. At the same time, we must see beyond micro deeds unto the macro deeds of Earthly balance (Eb). For it is not the unmerited warning of an alarmist, but a statement of ice-cold realism, to say that tidal wave after tidal wave of ecological collapse is approaching, which may soon be unavoidable and, once upon us, irreversible.

Eb shall redeem us. So, let us ever envision the long-range goal of {po + pbd + Ect + mbp}, which is, indeed, our divine summons to return to the Garden.

Chapter Four

The Probability of Success

WHAT are the chances that we can successfully implement Eb equaling {po + pbd + Ect + mbp} in some of our major cities?

First, {po}, which, as you recall, represents popular opinion, is essential to actualize the other three tasks symbolized in our formulaic expression. Indeed, informing the masses about the lifeless vacuum about to envelope us in an irreversible void is critical; however, we can also provide a solution—the futuristic vista of merit-based parenting {mbp} and its abounding benefits to all of life on Earth. We can tell them of the abundant life that a plant-based diet {pbd} holds for them and all the flora and fauna as well. We can envision for them the semi-paradise that our cities and countrysides will become as they are architecturally, spatially designed after the model of Earthly cities and transportation {Ect} and thus for living things rather than for the non-living automobile and its deadly path across the Earth. Indeed, public opinion is expedient. This means we must influence the popular viewpoint in our respective countries and cities, a feat that will be enhanced by four factors:

1. The present trend of ever-increasing individualism, a phenomenon of sovereignty, and, therefore, idiosyncratic thinking rather than thought-inhibiting propaganda distributed from centralized mind-benders, will allow {po} to be more easily influenced. *Truly* free thinking leads to the possibility of rationalism, opening just a crack in the door of lucidity, and the discourse of sobriety it piques. And no conversation is more lucid or more sobering than our message of Eb.

2. This same individualism, which has attracted nationalistic sentiments, is a prelude and reaction to a growing distrust of the media around the world, which is also a window of opportunity to herald our good news. As the droning mantra of the media creates an ever-widening backsliding of adherents, as more and more people reject it, we can own a niche within that gap, evangelistically filling it with hope.

3. What is more, we need only three percent of a na-

tional population for the impulsion needed to influence the remaining ninety-seven percent to follow our visionary lead. I feel we presently have those numbers.

4. And, quite simply, materializing Eb is probable because it is our singular polar star. We must realize it. It must be adapted, appearing in our day-to-day lives for our survival. There remain neither three paths nor two from which to choose. Only one.

Therefore, we are granted advantages to coalesce popular opinion by these four moments in the light.

The next subset in our equation is {pbd}, plant-based diet. According to the Food Revolution Network, "There's been a 600% increase in people identifying as vegans in the U.S. in the last three years. According to a report by research firm Global Data, only 1% of U.S. consumers claimed to be vegans in 2014. And in 2017, that number rose to 6%.

"In the UK, the number of people identifying as vegans has increased by 350%, compared to a decade ago, according to research commissioned by the Vegan Society in partnership with Vegan Life magazine.

"Veganism was a top search trend in Canada in 2017.

And the preliminary draft of Canada's new Food Guide, released in 2017 by the Canadian government, favors plant-based foods.

"In Portugal, vegetarianism rose by 400% in the last decade. This is according to research carried out by Nielsen.

"Plant-based diets are growing across Asia. New dietary guidelines released by the Chinese government encourage the nation's 1.3 billion people to reduce their meat consumption by 50%. Research predicts that China's vegan market will grow more than 17% between 2015 and 2020. In Hong Kong, 22% of the population reports practicing some form of a plant-based diet."

And the Executive V.P. of Strategic Business Units of Nestle, the world's largest food producer, says the plant-based diet is "on the rise."

Moreover, over one hundred doctors recently demonstrated peacefully in front of the White House to promote the plant-based diet. So, we might have neared and, in some regions, crossed the three percent threshold of this subset within our exegesis; thus, the probability of success here is quite high, for {pbd} is clearly a growth industry.

Next is {Ect}, Earthly cities and transportation. This is largely predicated upon subterranean travel that will, in the philosophy of architecture, be *formed* by the *function-*

ality of cities designed for living things rather than the inanimate automobile and the millions upon millions of acres of the life-entombing asphalt and concrete it requires.

Although not nearly as widely accepted as the plant-based diet, {Ect} is being planned, which resembles to my vision, especially subterranean transportation. Soon underground travel will be planned in precise concert with Earthly cities. To be sure, this futuristic symphony of human travel and human cities, both subordinate to nature, is forthcoming from the precious three percent of thinkers who join the vision of Eb.

In the meantime, people are developing ideas that are a prelude to {Ect}. Oslo, Norway, will ban all cars from its city center and replace thirty-five miles of roads with bike lanes. And, "Madrid plans to ban cars from 500 acres of its city center by 2020, with urban planners redesigning 24 of the city's busiest streets for walking rather than driving.

"The initiative is part of the Spanish capital's 'sustainable mobility plan,' which aims to reduce daily car usage from 29% to 23%." This is also a trend occurring in Berlin, New York, Belgium, Paris, San Francisco, London, Mexico City, Bogota, and many other cities.[46]

---

[46] Garfield, Leanna, "13 cities that are starting to ban cars,"(New York: Business Insider, 2018)

Now, {mbp}, which represents merit-based parenting, accents its alternative by frightful contrast: the diminishing quality of human life in relation to excessive population, a presage of slavery, despotic rule, as well as ongoing war for food, water, and land, pestilence, plague, and poverty. These are the unyielding accomplices to overpopulation. The most problematic of them, however, is the existential threat of ecological collapse, at which we are past the verge, for, as we have seen, 7.7 billion humans presently use 1.7 percent of the Earth's resources annually. Has our behavior, therefore, not transmuted from that of a fellow member of the flora and fauna to that of a parasite in the throes of killing its host?

As we have noted, this has driven the extinction rate above organic normality to an accelerated speed of death. What shall become of Earthly life in merely eight decades from this writing when human numbers may explode to a possible 11 billion hungry, thirsting, territorial consumers? Shall anyone but a fool assume that we, ourselves, are immune from this hellish juggernaut that, without feeling or remorse, runs over our lord's messengers, whom he has most graciously sent to redeem us?

Fate wields the terrible and swift avenging sword in one hand. In the other, she holds forth prosperity, health, peace, and the ability to recognize *value*, which is itself the state of love. She holds forth the garden, to which we are most openly invited to return.

Yet, we have the challenge of first influencing public opinion until merit-based parenting is socially accepted by the masses, at which time the majority will *want* it and the unprecedented quality of life it offers—prosperity, health, less crime, and higher achievements. Further details of its categoric implementation may be shortsighted to propose at this point in its evolution, especially within this writing. These will come in a series of reactions aligned with the acceptance of merit-based parenting as it unfolds organically and self-perpetually as it becomes the social norm. During this time, many individuals who possess a superior intellect will, together, conduct further thoughtwork about merit-based parenting's acceptance by the broad masses along with its day-to-day practice.

Simultaneously, we must expeditiously hasten the unfolding of this intrinsic subset of Eb, which is, as we have stressed, contingent upon public opinion {po}, which is further contingent upon the acceptable discourse of merit-based parenting {mbp}, itself. It must no longer be taboo among thinkers. We must move *the Overton window*, the window of socially permissible discussion, so that merit-based parenting can be weighed and examined dispassionately. This neither implies a move to the left nor to the right politically. 'Tis a step toward sanity, and this supersedes all partisan camps.

Consequently, merit-based parenting is the most urgent subset of our formula because: (1) it is presently a social anti-norm, whereas the other subsets are without an impeding taboo that will stop the growth of their acceptance. (2) And, {mbp} is urgent because an additional 2 billion people will succor the Earth's flora and fauna in only thirty years. So, we must move the Overton window toward the acceptance of a fair-minded dialogue about merit-based parenting.

In recapitulation of this chapter, public opinion {po} is increasingly favorable toward a plant-based diet {pbd} with a similar affinity for Earthly cities and transportation {Ect}, trends which apparently will continually increase over a long-range period.

Public opinion {po} may not, however, be ready to countenance merit-based parenting {mbp} with positive feelings or even open-mindedness. This is challenging and must be met as a welcomed opportunity for increasing discourse.

Therefore, with three out of four of our subsets (po, pbd, Ect) moving in a favorable direction, and with the other subset (mbp) merely having unknown public acceptability, which we can change, if necessary, I feel that Eb's probability of success is quite reasonable. Of course, this is with the full understanding that we have decades of smart, hard work ahead of us. Yet, with an honest fight, I believe we shall win.

These are some of the things we might do to be part of the three percent who lead the world, further increasing our probability of success:

Begin at the only beginning—your inner ecosystem. Eat more foods from the plant-based diet {pbd} until you are eating only unprocessed food that grows on plants. It's perfectly fine to ease into this life-giving menu over time. You might want to begin by enjoying a big salad every day filled with multi-colored vegetables. The more colors, the more nutrients you will receive. Try the recipes I provided. Your health will improve, and others might want to know how you did it and why you look so good, which may be a good time to share the plant-based diet with them.

Adherents of Eb might conduct research about Earthly cities and transportation {Ect} and, upon gathering enough facts, publish scholarly papers about it. You needn't be a student, of course. Those who are retired are excellent candidates for projects such as this. If you are, however, a student, consider studying to become a city planner who specializes in {Ect}. We will need to call upon your expertise soon. In the meantime, be bold and inventive, pressing the envelope of orthodox city plans and transport to align with Eb. As you do, remember that once our transportation aligns with nature, the appropriate formation of our cities will follow.

Think about merit-based parenting {mbp}, its manifold benefits to humankind, and the rest of the Earth's flora and fauna. Should you be a student, write papers about {mbp}, expounding upon its ability to usher in a quality of Earthly life hitherto unknown throughout "the long and winding road" of history. You may even become a much-needed expert on this all-important subject, eventually helping to save the world from the perils of overpopulation. Should anyone condemn you for suggesting merit-based parenting {mbp}, politely and courteously enlighten them by stating that contraceptives such as birth control pills are quite clearly negative birth control yet are widely accepted around the world.

Unlike traditional contraceptives, however, {mbp} eases economic burdens, replacing them with robust economic freedom. It reduces crime and, possibly, changes the warring character of whole regions to one of peace. It provides a competitive environment conducive for frequenter and higher achievement. It improves health by eliminating an array of congenital diseases. It christens human life with a hallmark of high worth, with each birth being an occurrence of comparatively greater value than is realized today. Furthermore, {mbp} vitally reduces human encroachment upon the flora and fauna, in turn, halting and reversing ecological collapse as no other remedy may provide.

As you do these things, begin to practice the ten good ecological deeds we discussed.

1. Eating a plant-based diet
2. Driving less
3. Recycling
4. Composting
5. Planting a garden
6. Planting trees
7. Feeding wild birds
8. Avoiding commercial cleaning products
9. Using less energy
10. Using less water

You may wish to reread the particulars of these good deeds, which we discussed earlier.

As you go about promoting $\{po + pbd + Ect + mbp\} = Eb$ and doing these ten necessary good turns, always conduct yourself with dignity and courtesy, behaving as ladies and gentlemen. Always carefully, even meticulously, obey the law, being especially respectful to law enforcement and government officials. If you organize a demonstration, you must obtain all the needed permits well in advance of the event. And it must be a *silent* demonstration, only talking among yourselves and answering questions should a passerby make an inquiry. Of course, we must never block pedestrian or automobile traffic or interfere with a business. For you are representing the blessed flora and fauna and must behave with corresponding dignity.

And as you do, remember the rubric of our victory: rather than fighting *against* toxic ideologies and systems, we are fighting *for* life-giving, futuristic ideas that shall cause the obsolescence of the former.

Chapter Five

An Intimate and Revealing Interview

Please note that redundant and inarticulate expressions, often used during informal conversations, are edited from this interview, making it pleasanter to read.

Hardcastle:
Thank you, Mr. Hathaway, for being with us.

Hathaway:
My pleasure, of course. Just call me Phillip.

Hardcastle:
Thank you. Is your diet completely plant-based?

Hathaway:
Yes. One hundred percent. All plant-based.

Hardcastle:

A lot of people say they're plant-based but eat fish, dairy, or even chicken. But you don't eat any of those things. Is that right?

Hathaway:

Correct. No animals or things that come from them. I've yet to find the fish tree or the cheese tree.

Hardcastle:

[Laughter] Yes. Lots of people eat fish and cheese while claiming to be plant-based. What inspired you to adopt a plant-based diet?

Hathaway:

I went to a retreat that was all vegetarian several years ago, and that's what drew me closer. It was an epiphany. But getting to an all-plant menu was a process that took a few years.

Hardcastle:
Why a few years?

Hathaway:

Had I known how horribly dairy cows are treated, I would have become plant-based right away. I wish I had learned about this sooner. You know, well . . . we're all on separate learning curves. Each one of us. We learn something in this area, then something else in that area, and so on. All just crawling towards the light, so to speak.

Hardcastle:
Because you're plant-based, some readers will want to know about your weight.

Hathaway:
Of course. This morning I was 166 lbs. I'm six feet tall.

Hardcastle:
How long at that weight? And how do you feel?

Hathaway:
Ten years [at this weight]. Full of vigor and vim and optimism.

Hardcastle:
What's your secret to staying fit?

Hathaway:
Plant-based food, no junk food, no bread, crackers, cookies, no drinking, no smoking, no medications whatsoever, not even aspirin or ibuprofen. And, daily light exercise.

Heavier workouts three times a week. But all the exercise in the world won't keep you fit if you're not eating correctly.

By the way, those on the plant-based diet should take a daily B-complex and protein supplement. These are superior to animal sources of vitamin B and protein.

Hardcastle:
You don't mention global warming [in your book]. Why?

Hathaway:
The equation unites both camps that debate climate change and global warming against a common foe—a more perilous foe, which is, of course, the detonative population. There are beautiful, courageous people on both sides of that debate, and I hope in the future they'll work together against the greater existential threat of overpopulation. This is dearly needed if we expect to see progress

Incidentally, I am neither a Democrat nor a Republican, liberal nor conservative. Also, the equation is not associated in any way with the Green New Deal or United Nations Agenda 21. The equation is elegantly simple by comparison, without a tangled labyrinth of bureaucracy. Think of Beethoven's *Fifth Symphony*. With four notes, he built a celestial city of musical grandeur. Likewise, the four notes of the equation have the potential to create a new world.

Hardcastle:
The best solutions tend to be quite simple ones. Now, what inspired you to write this book?

Hathaway:
Oh, well . . . I'm flooded with answers. Hmmm . . . Let's see. All right, I suppose a concise answer is beauty. Simply beauty. For the sake of beauty.

The irreducible answer, however, is *the recognition of value,* which is my definition of love in its purest sense. Writing this book is my very humble way to save the beautiful. Before this can be done, the value of beauty must be recognized. In other words, beauty must be loved.

So, I wrote this book to inspire others to recognize value, which is the most elementary act of love. And, nothing exceeds the value of our bodies and the infinite miracles we call Earth. The equation is my humble contribution to the awakening to their absolute value. Yet who am I? I am merely a constituent particle in a galaxy spinning towards its completion.

Hardcastle:
Your poem, "The Battle of Earth", which is in your fore-word. I think the line that struck me most . . . Well, it's two lines:

"Yet a remnant saw them a war waging,
In flashes of light against the darkness,"

It's as though we're in darkness, and we see what is truly happening in flashes of light against the darkness all around us. And this causes an awakening from human-kind's catatonic slumber. It reminds me of "Sleepers Awake!" by Bach.

Which seems to be thematic in your book. The same idea came to mind when you wrote about Plato's allegory of the cave, where people could only see shadows of what was happening in the real world and that the flora and fauna are but a foretaste of things to come.

Hathaway:
Yes. "For now, we see through a glass, darkly; but then face to face." It's a slow awakening. We are so, so far from harmony with the flora and fauna, lost in darkness. But they [the flora and fauna] are gifts of light. Like standing before a painting you've studied in school and seen in magazines, and then one day you see the original.

The details and colors are incomparably more vivid and robust. It was like that when I saw *The Night Watch* by Rembrandt. This, too, is a gift of light. All these gifts come from the artistry of light. From the true master of light and dark.

Hardcastle:
Why the battle theme?

Hathaway:
I simply used the battle metaphorically. I'm a pacifist. I feel it's appropriate [to use a battle metaphorically] because just look at the oceanic change we propose to affect. It's titanic. Global. And, it will be met with intense resistance as those of antiquated thinking dig in their heels, fighting [against] their own salvation. So, it's a battle, indeed.

Of course, I feel that the pen is mightier than the sword. Though I use the metaphor of a battle, Earthly balance {Eb}, of course, is *never, never* something we force upon people, no more than a grocer forces people to buy his food. They *want* his food. People needn't be forced to buy shoes, they *want* them.

Likewise, people will want the prosperity, the peaceable quietness of the neighborhoods, the precious peace with virtually no war, the sheer beauty of their green cities, where they enjoy crystal clear water and pristine air and [fruit and vegetable] produce rich with vitamins and minerals, and the life-giving health all this provides. They will want a city, nation, and world where life is highly esteemed, and therefore, where they, themselves, will be esteemed more than ever before in human history. Suffering will be eased. A new epoch of humankind, of all Earthly life.

Hardcastle:
Do you really believe that?

Hathaway:
Why shouldn't I? We must think boldly and act boldly upon that thinking. If one loves something, he wants the absolute best for it, doesn't he? Of course. And I love the flora and fauna, of which we are members. If someone loves something, he is willing to fight for it, isn't he? Yes. I and the other three percent are willing to fight to save Earthly life. Wouldn't it be blasphemous to not do so? That is why I created the equation.

Hardcastle:
Let's talk about Giles Pison. He's is an anthropologist, a demographer, and professor at the National Museum of Natural History, and associate researcher at the French

Institute for Demographic Studies, a research institute specializing in demography and population studies. [He is a] very respected man. He says the high estimate for the year 2100 is 16 billion people. You reference him in your book. What do you think of his high estimation?

Hathaway:
Well, one thing is certain, no one knows what will happen in 2100. We have a pretty good handle on 2050 projections. Beyond that, however, is speculative. I feel we should expect the best and prepare for the worst. It could be a deadly situation. That's why I created the equation, each subset of which is essential in order to avoid the high estimate and possibly curtail the estimate of 11 billion human souls by 2100.

Yet, I feel that the moderate projection of 11 billion for 2100 is weak simply because we must have a fanciful expectation of zero population growth in all regions except Sub-Sahara Africa. This theory depends upon various factors, but principally urbanization.

There are, however, vast megacities in Sub-Sahara Africa, and this has not deterred the geometric growth of their populace. So, it appears to me that 11 billion is optimistically low, since it is predicated upon the assumption of zero population growth in the rest of the world. I pray that I'm wrong.

Hardcastle:
Great segue to my next question. You refer to the divine occasionally in *The Hathaway Equation*. Are you religious?

Hathaway:
I'm not at all religious. But at the same time, I believe in, or, rather, [I] *know* God. It's like this. Children may believe in Santa Claus, yet this belief is often a hope fraught with doubt, which would be utterly dismissed by meeting and further knowing Herr Claus.

Likewise, isn't one's belief in God, which requires continuous bolstering by a daily renewal of faith, inferior to meeting and knowing God? I know him through a super-sensual knowing, an awareness in messages within the flora and fauna themselves. Of course, this doesn't make me unique, for everyone receives the same missives. It's not as though I'm seeing visions or hearing voices.

Hardcastle:
[Laughter] I love your sense of humor. But what about things that aren't so divine? Here's something I'd like to read that Sir David Attenborough said.

"My response is that when Creationists talk about God creating every individual species as a separate act, they always instance hummingbirds, or orchids, sunflowers and beautiful things. But I tend to think instead of a parasitic worm that is boring through the eye of a boy sitting on the bank of a river in West Africa, [a worm] that's going to make him blind. And [I ask them], 'Are you telling me that the God you believe in, who you also say is an all-merciful God, who cares for each one of us individually, are you saying that God created this worm that can live in no other way than in an innocent child's eyeball? Because that doesn't seem to me to coincide with a God who's full of mercy.'"

Hathaway:
Now I am just another traveler. That is all. Yet, it seems that Sir David poses a valuable question that helps us learn. The lesson is quite simple, really. Just as there are good and bad people, there are good and harmful organisms. Some are vessels of light, some of darkness, others of variant shadows and light diffused in the battle of good and evil. We want to be with the people of light. Not darkness. We want to be with the organisms that are vessels of light—life-giving organisms and good bacteria. Not those like this parasitic worm that was an ambassador of darkness, so to speak.

In other words, it is the light that we must focus upon and

to which we must be drawn, not only the flora and fauna themselves. This aligns with quantum physics, as I have read. For from beginning to end, we are light particles—an autobiographical mosaic of light particles comprised of all we have seen, heard, sensed, or experienced in any way. And with these, we wage war against the darkness.

Yet on the spectrum of light and darkness, we are typically gray, hopefully light gray. Yet, the tones and tints change with peaks and valleys. But should we *artificially* venture too far to the light, we, like Icarus, may fall headlong and tragically from precipitous heights. We must be humble. Humble yet lionhearted. Who can do this? We must try. It's not easy.

So, it's only natural that we want to be with the fauna who possess a superhuman ability to love and forgive, for kindness and gentleness. They comfort us. My dear flat-coated retriever, Blackjack, taught me more about these than all the priests and prophets and swamis of this world. The flora also holds regular lessons about all these things, you know. Free tuition, no books to read or essays to write.

Now, back to the supersensual that we were discussing. What we perceive as the creation, perhaps the Darwinian creation, is not evidence of a creator. This seems a contradiction. Yet, embodied within the inexhaustible variations of what I and many others call the creation, or the Darwinian creation, is the message—the repetitious message spoken without words, without end, and with the warmest smile of friendship: *Peace, life, love, dear friend.* I hasten to say that these ideas are clearly not from a position of religiosity. I don't promote religions or new age ideas or humanism, neither do I get involved in occultism nor anything that resembles it.

Hardcastle:
It does sound something like deism.

Hathaway:
No, deism is the belief in the divine because of reason and nature, on neither of which I hang my hat.

Hardcastle:
Aren't you hanging your hat on nature?

Hathaway:
Not ultimately. Well . . . for the sake of clarity, it may be helpful to explain my view of the Universe. It's really not *my* view. It's merely a view of the beautiful. You know, some people will challenge my idea that the flora and

fauna are representational of the divine. So, maybe this would be the right place to explain it.

Well, first of all, we, the finite, can possess an inexplicable knowing but never a truly academic understanding of the Infinite. Anemic attempts to do so by certain religious philosophers and scholars is oftentimes "much ado about nothing," being little more than inventive, yet certainly well-intended, gyrations of wasteful energy. Instead, let's assume a Socratic approach to understand what little we may about the everlasting.

What causes the human heart to beat rhythmically while yet in the womb and continue to do so with almost perfect cadence for possibly a century? It is electrical impulses, of course. What causes these electrical pulsations in us and, simultaneously, in untold trillions of other living beings? No one knows. Yet, mightn't they all arise in a cacophony that, at some point in its global pulsations, becomes symphonic vibrations? If so, perhaps that is where nature finds its tune.

Hardcastle:
That seems logical since all things are vibrations, even light waves.

Hathaway:
Precisely. And what causes Earth to travel around the Sun, its gravitational pull counterbalancing Earth's centrifugal force so that it travels in predictable orbit? This is analogous, say physicists, to a central nucleus having several electrons revolving around it in mutual electric attractions, all within a given atomic boundary.

And, the electric force of the electrons and the gravitational force of Earth possess further similarities. They vary in inverse proportion to the squared distance from the hub of their orbit. The centers of their orbits are the nucleus and Sun, respectively. This results in the *same* type of elliptic orbit as Earth to Sun and electron to nucleus. In other words, nucleoli and electrons are subatomic replicas of our solar system.

Hardcastle:
Amazing. Simply amazing. Same orbit.

Hathaway:
Right. So, aren't these examples of the hand of God?

Hardcastle:
I would think so.

Hathaway:
Well, perhaps not. That was a rhetorical question, by the way, so please don't think I was trying to trap you.

Hardcastle:
No, no. I didn't feel that way.

Hathaway:
Good. Well, Immanuel Kant, the Prussian-German theological philosopher, might say this wonderworking of the Universe is merely evidence of an architect rather than a creator, or perhaps, just as easily the creation of the whole by the parts themselves. Because within the exact parameters of dispassionate logic, design does not necessarily imply designer, since we might project our notion of design into the Universe, attempting to attribute our mundane version of common sense to it.

From that point, we often project an image of its Poet who, lo and behold, looks much like us! Creating God in man's image—an *anthropomorphic* portrayal of the divine. Desperately, we thus seek our own importance.

So, many philosophies do little more than repetitiously redress the argument of design therefore designer. Yet, whether the design is explained scientifically, mathematically, philosophically, or religiously, none can prove the existence of God. Yet, there remains a supersensual knowing, one that is *a priori*; in other words, it is inferred and rational, transcending terrestrial logic. For the subject upon which all else is predicated is infinitesimal, whereas we are finite and limited by mortal thoughts.

Therefore, the subatomic replication of Earth's orbit 'round the Sun and untold phenomena like this are not logical evidence of God's hand but messages with spiritual content transcending sensual knowledge alone, penetrating our poor, darkened hearts with light unseen. Thus, it is perhaps an appropriate spiritual boundary to view nature as our divine window and, thereby, without further theological explanation, to *know*.

Hardcastle:
Fascinating. But how do you *know* you know?

Hathaway:
[Laughter] Well, please remember that I am not religious, although what I'm about to say sounds like it. One day, I knew someone was praying for me. I knew it just as surely as I know that I am sitting here talking with you. I didn't need to read ancient and esoteric manuscripts. I didn't need to sing hymns to know this.

Neither did I need to visit what is considered by others to be a holy place. I didn't need to chant, or touch prayer beads, or dance and beat drums. I didn't need to burn incense, or go to a monastery. I didn't need to seek out a holy man, or priest or a prophet. I simply knew just like I know we're sitting here talking.

A short time after that experience, just a few days, without seeking the information at all, I was told that this person was praying fervently for me at the very time—the very time I suddenly became aware of it. I feel all of us have a similar knowing about the flora and fauna. We know who they are. But many suppress this knowing, which imperils the soul.

Hardcastle:
So, you feel we can nurture our souls without being religious or without religion, at all. Is that what I understand you to say? It's kind of like learning to ride [a bike] without training wheels. Right?

Hathaway:
Yes. Training wheels is a good simile. I feel we've been given all the messages we need within the flora and fauna. That is why halting and reversing ecological collapse is so important to me. We must listen to and learn from the flo-

ra and fauna, not kill them. They're divine messages to us. Personal messages to each of us as individuals.

Hardcastle:
If I hear you, physical health opens the door to spiritual health. Or should I say the plant-based diet does this?

Hathaway:
Correct. The plant-based diet is an experience of conscious awareness. I hope my soul is strengthened day by day despite my many, many weaknesses, and so I trust the spirit of my soul grows and this miraculously rather than of my own doing. Again, this is nothing at all unique. It's the same process for everyone. You know, it's funny. People often talk of being spiritual as though it's exceptional. Yet, it's as meaningless as though they declared, *I have a nose.*

Most people have a nose, of course. Likewise, everyone has a spirit. Some clean, some in need of cleaning. Some good, some in need of goodness. The point is that everyone is spiritual simply because everyone has a spirit, which is the condition of the soul.

Hardcastle:
The big question is: how do we care for our soul?

Hathaway:
I think the plant-based diet may be the best start. From this [point], being a good steward of the flora and fauna becomes an almost involuntary, intuitive response, I feel. And this is the path to growth, spiritual growth, which is evidence of the soul's revival and health.

We know a plant is healthy according to its blossom and greenness, for these represent the condition of the life within the plant. Likewise, we know a person is healthy according to what radiates from him or her since this is also the condition of the soul.

Hardcastle:
Intriguing. So, the spirit is the condition of the soul. They're two different things?

Hathaway:
Yes. That's right. Now, let me be quick to add that I still lose my temper with the electric company for billing me incorrectly. I'm no saint. No better than anyone else. And, it seems every time I feel I'm growing spiritually, one of these overcharges from the phone company comes along or I receive abysmal customer service, which I can barely endure. Sometimes I think of Jean Valjean [the protagonist of *Les Misérables* by Victor Hugo] who endured so much suffering, and feel I'm only standing in the shadow of this full measure of a man.

Hardcastle:
Now, you wrote this book to save beauty. Is that right?

Hathaway:
Well, there is a beauty that is all-inclusive. It is all the beauty. I, of course, don't propose to save all beauty. That would be ridiculous. I'm not that influential [laughter]. Neither do I propose to save all the flora and fauna. I suppose some of them will survive no matter what I or others do. I only hope to put forth a plan, one that is quite simple, mind you, to halt and reverse ecological demise over the coming decades. This certainly won't happen fast. It will only be accomplished with millions of like-minded people around the world. *The recognition of value is the key. Indeed, it is the key to the door of the equation.*

So, I hope . . . it is my hope that we will halt and reverse the collapse of the ecosystem. And this is an important nuance of that hope, so I want to say this with some emphasis and clarity. *It is wrong, morally wrong, to not have this hope.* In other words, this is how we should think. With hope. We should be thinking in terms of "this is how we will do this." Can do, positive thought. When we consider the inexpressibly beautiful world—the abundantly beautiful world that was bequeathed to us—isn't it an abomination to be unwilling to save it?

Those who recognize value are the willing few. In other words, those who love.

Hardcastle:
How do we reach those who simply don't care?

Hathaway:
We must separate deed from doer, disapproving of the deed yet loving the doer. I feel that adopting this peacemaking mentality is the only path to triumph. Now, for the sake of further disambiguation, because this point is so important—anyone is welcome to disagree with me or Eb. I expect them to do so. I will still respect them, of course. I certainly won't hate or dislike them for disagreeing with me. In fact, I often find it easy to be friends with those with whom I disagree or who disagree with me.

Disagreement can foster friendship. This is so merely because disagreement may cause some degree of empathy, which is a kindhearted temperament. Open disagreement is also an act of honesty. However, it's best to do so politely. What to have for dinner, or what music to listen to, or where to go on vacation aren't so important. There are bigger issues before us all. Yet, even these bigger issues should cause empathetic feelings [when others disagree with us about them].

For example, it's obvious that I feel very strongly about redeeming the environment. And, many will disagree that this is even an issue. Many will say it cannot be done at all. This is wrong thinking. And wrong thinking can be destructive. For example, disbelieving that we can halt and reverse ecological collapse is the antithesis of faith. Yet, at the same time, I offer those who disbelieve [that we can halt and reverse ecological collapse] a hand up in true and genuine friendship. Because it's absurd, you know, to expect everyone to be at the same point of awareness. Kindness and patience combined with persistence wins the day. It's not always easy to be this patient. Yet, we must try.

So, to go back to your question—*how do we reach those who don't care about the flora and fauna?*

Hardcastle:
Good. Yes. This is a of great importance I would think to effect public policy.

Hathaway:
Right, public opinion. First, we must be patient with them. We must realize that we are all on a learning curve. Secondly, we must do the ten good deeds. They help all living things, and doing them also encourages others to do them. This is a timely mindset that I hope takes root

amidst the contentious strife swirling round debates about the ecosystem.

For I admire members of both camps, and it grievously disappoints me to see them attack each other, conjuring up negativity while wasting energy that should be focused with laser-beam intensity on the real issues. Perhaps chief among them [the real issues] is the population syndrome—the brontosaurus at the tea party, which it seems is seldom acknowledged.

Being purely numerical and exceedingly vast, however, it is a beast easily spotted and impossible to deny logically as it sits at our table. It may be assumed that the dangers of overpopulation in ratio to the food supply should be foremost in our minds as we think of this cumbersome guest.

Hardcastle:
A problem so big that no one can ignore it. You wrote a poem about it that you just mentioned in passing, titled, "The Brontosaurus at the Tea Party".

Hathaway:
[Yes, it is] a lighthearted innuendo of the reluctance to discuss the overbearing issue.

Hardcastle:
Back to the subject of beauty. Would you say that halting and reversing ecological collapse is a by-product of saving beauty?

Hathaway:
That's right. When we see the beauty all around us—so much beauty—we become the wealthiest of all people. You know, I am told that some of the richest people in the world are quite miserable. I feel this may be because of their limited ability to see beauty, perhaps because it's something they assume can be purchased.

Yet, seeing and appreciating beauty is genuine wealth and riches. If I had all the gold in the world—every bit of it—and could never again see the beautiful, I would be a dreadfully lost soul. And, we are losing beauty so rapidly due to humankind's ignorance. Beautiful lives . . . beautiful lives of the flora and fauna, visually beautiful lives who are not only beautiful to behold but who live in beautiful ways. Even their ways are beautiful.

The most intelligent way, my strategy to save them, is to introduce people to a healthy lifestyle. A healthy way of living that, as a natural result, extends to the world all about them as we . . . together become good stewards of the flora and fauna. So, we see . . . that personal health and ecological stewardship are correlative terms.

Hardcastle:
If I hear you correctly, you're saying only those who are healthy will be good stewards of the Earth. Is that right?

Hathaway:
No, indeed. Some, of course, have lost their health due to circumstances beyond their control. On the other hand, some extremely health-conscious people are rather reckless about the world outside themselves. So, it's more accurate to say that those who are taking good care of their health, the best they can, will be *more likely* to care for the Earth.

For example, if you have someone who eats junk food all day while watching television and is very slothful, it seems *most unlikely* that he would, in opposition to the way he cares for himself, diligently care for the flora and fauna. Whereas, he who is a good steward of himself will have a greater tendency to care for the Earthly life all about him. That is why I gave such consideration to personal health [in this book].

Hardcastle:
Would it be right to say that you wrote *The Hathaway*

Equation to save beauty?

Hathaway:
Yes. But that answer in and of itself may be misleading. As you recall, you asked what inspired it's writing, and I said beauty. Obviously, I wrote it to stop and reverse ecological collapse and this involves many things. One of them is to ease suffering. There is so much suffering in the world and we must be attuned to it. We mustn't turn our backs on those who are suffering, whether they be the human or nonhuman members of the creation.

Hardcastle:
Tell us about Nidhi.

Hathaway:
Yes, I will. But first, let me say this about suffering. I'm not, you know, suggesting that we walk around sad all the time. We should be positive and upbeat most of the time. Yet, our lives were not given to us . . . this marvel, which is our lives and the limitless miracles all about us, were not granted to us only that we might have fun. This is what is called a thrill seeker, and these people often never accomplish anything, wasting all the opportunities that come to them. So, we need to be positive and have fun. True. That is, if we don't ignore suffering, which is en-

dured by the multitudes like Nidhi. The name means "my treasure," as you may recall.

Hardcastle:
Does it trouble you to talk about her?

Hathaway:
In a bittersweet way. She's a jewel in my heart. Purely platonic, of course. As you remember from reading the story [in this book], I only caught a glimpse of her for a few seconds when on a train in India, pulling away from the turnstile where she had just arrived. Yet my thoughts of her seem to become more vividly clear over the years. I guess it's more accurate to say that the memory doesn't change but becomes more poignant. Indelibly.

You know, my heartrending thoughts of her ultra-feminine facial features smitten by the fact that she had missed the train and the passengers she had hoped to beg of. Just so brave amid the horror that she must endure. The fact that she had so carefully arranged her hair and the ribbon in it and her matching pretty dress and yet missed the train and all those [from whom] she hoped to receive a few gifts of mercy. So, the equation, particularly the subset {mbp} [merit-based parenting] will, I truly believe, cause many of these cases of unimaginable sufferings to become nightmarish relics of a crude epoch in history.

Hardcastle:
What will happen if your equation is not implemented? Do you feel that we can live without it?

Hathaway:
Superb question. Alright now, let's give this some thought. This is a way to look at it and an accurate way, I believe. Any living thing must move to continue living. We, for example, may have enough water, food, air, and shelter. But, if we could not move, our circulatory system, respiratory system, and our lymph node system would begin to degenerate, and this atrophy would affect the vital organs, as well. Living in this atrophic state would soon be fatal.

Now, human society is also a living organism, so to speak. And, at this point in its societal evolution, it has become stale and stagnant. It is not moving. In other words, it's not evolving. Here, I do not mean Darwinian evolution. The evolution I am speaking of is purely societal.

Yet, this society is not evolving. And, in eighty years it may have reached 11 billion souls. Many ecologists and scientists feel this is unsustainable and will be ruthlessly readjusted by nature without mercy in the form of famine, plagues, pestilence, and wars. These could come suddenly

and globally for nature shall not long countenance an in-
terloper within her garden. Then, *then* shall come the
Darwinian adjustment.

Earthly balance (Eb) is the merciful and intelligent alternative to nature's implacable vengeance.

"So, look well to thyself, I say, or ill may befall thee . . .
When the flood cometh, it sweepeth away grain as well as
chaff."

Hardcastle:
Shakespeare?

Hathaway:
From the writings of the prolific author and artist Howard
Pyle. One of my favorites.

So, Earthly balance expressed in (Eb) is the thing, the
plan to enliven the human species into life-giving movement with a certain *élan* heretofore unknown among men.
This is the movement we want, not plague, pestilence, and
pandemonium. Consequently, purely from a safety stand-
point, which must be the foremost concern of every
nation's leader, the equation should be given judicious
thought since it will save humankind from approaching

environmental calamities.

 Sub-Sahara Africa, for example, is presently the only world region that is a population time bomb waiting to detonate. With it comes multiplied diseases, illiteracy, consanguinity, and thus more corruption and war. Sub-Sahara Africa needs the equation dearly. To implement it there, however, it must be accepted in the West, the preeminent importer of innovation. So, we must first change the way *we* think.

You know, yesterday I heard an influential political pundit say that we'll never have a shortage of resources because the greatest human resource is the mind, which can create anything. Yet, the only tools the mind has at its disposal to implement its visions come from Earth. From what would this pundit create oxygen? From what food and water? From what warmth and energy?

Look in the sky and see the huge jet. It came from the mind of men. But each part and piece of that jet—the steel, aluminum, copper, plastic, glass, and its fuel—was extracted from Earth. Think of this when you see a jet, a skyscraper, or a gigantic oil tanker. It came from the Earth, a finite resource. Not only from our minds.

I feel this is very important to remember. So, we have many people like this political commentator who are alienated from Earth who feel they can conjure anything into existence by conceiving it with never the concern for natural resources. And, it's our job to influence them to consider new and far, far better possibilities.

Hardcastle:
How long do you anticipate this taking?

Hathaway:
Acceptance of Eb will take decades. But we must make giant strides in the next thirty years before things get so far out of control that they can't be reined in. The horizon, however, is bright with promise since the plant-based diet, which is integral to the equation, is becoming more and more widely accepted. Lots of people are talking about it.

It's funny, too, that it's much like a religion in that everyone . . . or I should say, many people, want to outdo others by piously bragging about the plant-based diet. It's vogue. It's fashion. That's good if most of those people are actually eating plant-based. It's as though . . . Well, if we may, let's go back to your question about the acceptability of Eb [Earthly balance] and the time it will take to become pervasive. Would that be alright?

Hardcastle:
Please.

Hathaway:
So, how long it will take to become pervasive in just one world region? Twenty-five to fifty years. I assume the epicenter will be Sub-Sahara Africa. I assume this is where it will [begin] based on statistics, this will be the beachhead of Eb. Europe is where the Overton window will open, nonetheless.

From there, it will be exported to Africa, where it will be implemented. Of course, the Overton window is the socially accepted narrative of Eb. And, this will move in our favor in correlation to the awareness of ecological malaise. Publicity regarding the unparalleled, cataclysmic events developing in Africa. [Or] the island of plastic floating in the Pacific . . .

Hardcastle:
Possibly the size of Texas, right?

Hathaway:
I believe it's three times the size of Texas or France. Such a tragedy! Such a horrible tragedy! This harbinger of doom is, in turn, a warning signal. Turning a problem into an opportunity. The more we hear of these catastrophes, the more the Overton window will most likely move in our favor. So, we always must turn these ecological trag-

edies into opportunities to present Eb [Earthly balance] as the overarching solution . . . one in which everybody wins economically, socially, with individual health, happiness, and peace.

As I see it, this good message will grow in Europe and export to the African countries where the population explosions are occurring. These are the regions that need it the most. So, as in the long wagon train of history, Europe will lead the nations of the world to Earthly balance, the right side of our equation symbolized as {Eb}. Although I feel there will be considerable interest in India since they are keen to maintain a zero-population growth rate. I feel this will all take twenty-five to fifty years.

Hardcastle:
This brings up an important issue that I almost forgot. I have research that was conducted regarding the percentages of IQ levels. According to this analysis . . . I'm reading my notes . . . by the year 2050, it is projected that seventy-eight percent (78%) of the population will have an IQ of less than 100. So, this means that if we have a population of 11 billion by 2050, which may be a conservative estimate, there will be 8.6 billion people with an IQ of less than 100.

To compound the problem, twenty-six percent (26%) or 2.8 billion people are predicted to have an IQ of 70 or less. But it gets worse. There is a scarcity of those who are very bright—it is forecasted that less than one percent (1%) will possess an IQ of 130.[47]

How will merit-based parenting affect over three quarters of Earth's population who have IQs of less than 100? How it will impact over one-quarter of those with less than 70?

Hathaway:
This is quite tragic and, I feel, unnecessary. Characteristically, those in this segment of the population—those with an IQ of under 100—are less able to see the full set of variables in day-to-day decision-making processes. They tend to think in short-term gratification, take less care of their bodies, and the environment; they have a propensity to argue unnecessarily and have children during adolescence and out of wedlock.

Sadly, these innate behavior patterns assure negligent parenting, which perpetuates misery. And, that's seventy-eight percent of the population. It's equally distressing that less than one percent will possess an IQ of 130 or

---

[47] Lynn, Richard and Tatu Vanhanen, *IQ and the Wealth of Nations*. (Westport: Praeger, 2002)

higher, which is our world's repository of inventiveness and foresight.

Well, my response is theoretical, of course, yet under the guidance of the equation, a higher percentage of these people will disqualify themselves from parenthood. It's essential, however, to remember this: the disqualifying factor will be behavior rather than one's respective IQ.

The word behavior is critical. In other words, I'm certain that, for example, if someone has an IQ of 95, shall we say . . . I don't feel that would inhibit—or maybe a better word might be *prevent* him or her from being a model citizen and qualifying for the privilege of parenthood. Those who do qualify will experience an unprecedented improvement in every aspect of their lives because, as you know, the most downtrodden will benefit the most from {mbp}.

Now, I feel it's paramount to keep {mbp} in perspective. First, it's about managing the population—not about interfering with people's lives. It should be as unobtrusive as possible. What is more, it's not perfect. We may assume there will be latent functions associated with {mbp} such as the possibility of increased promiscuity since participating males will be at least temporarily infertile. How will this affect the institution of marriage, morals, and subsequently, society? Will a necessary ratio of individuals find {mbp} attractive? We simply don't know.

I feel, however, that many people wish to live without children. As we've discussed, many people, especially those in regions racked by intense poverty, dread the birth of their children; many in the wealthy nations feel similarly yet find themselves with children, nonetheless. This is heartbreaking. Calamitous to themselves, their children, and society.

All the wisdom of Pericles cannot exceed the savvy of this one admonition: fathers, mothers, lovingly hold your babies close to your breasts. Sing to them, gently acknowledge their wigglings, for these are urgent signals for help—your help that only you can give.

Their animations of longing must be exchanged with paternal and maternal gesticulations of kindness, an interchange, which must occur seamlessly—at least many times each waking hour for the first five years of baby's life. The damage perpetrated without these life-giving acknowledgements is irredeemable—a permanent stamp upon the infant's unconscious mind that can never be erased.

Consequently, while merit-based parenting is primarily a population management methodology, it simultaneously broadens and deepens the base and incidence of good parenting. This subset of the equation, along with the other three subsets, may turn our present dark disarray into golden daybreak. That's the whole purpose of Eb, *to turn this environmental quandary into an opportunity,* in which we assume our proper place among the flora and fauna.

Hardcastle:
Is that the one thing you want your readers to come away with after reading *The Hathaway Equation?* Turning ecological collapse into an opportunity to usher in a new era?

Hathaway:
Yes, that is the intended effect. Yes, exactly.

Hardcastle:
In addition to that, what else?

Hathaway:
Hmm . . . I think . . . well, you know I think it would be three things. First, we are not the crown of creation with royal prerogatives over the king's other subjects, but fellow members of the same kingdom of flora and fauna all

meant to serve the great king by caring for his creation.

Secondly, the equation will bring economic freedom, health, safety, social refinement, and dignity to the poorest people. It will, by nature, bring this to all people whether rich or poor. And, [third] of course, it will be a recrudescence of the flora and fauna.

Hardcastle:
The "second coming" of the flora and fauna, as you said, which is a wonderful thought.

Many, many thanks for your time today. It's gone by quickly and there's much more I'd like to talk about. Didn't even get to your visions for cities and travel. But it's been fascinating, futuristic, even iconoclastic. Before we end, are there any other closing thoughts you'd like to share with us?

Hathaway:
The first thing that comes to mind is our starry future. We won't get there through eugenics. Our pathway to the stars is good parenting.

And, please keep this ever-present within your mind—someone else will not fix the problem. You, dear listener [or reader], must be the solution. Be the example that inspires others. Let those virtues exude from you which you wish to see in others.

This brings us to another important point. Do not expect the solution to come from the government. The pure governmental expression of the equation might be one of force.

Rather, the equation must be a new set of social standards—standards much loftier than those we labor under today. Social norms that are freely chosen because they are superior to the former way that is now exhausted.

Earth can endure it no longer.

For the law of survival is the highest law, overlording all others. We obey it or perish.

But be of good cheer. The first three subsets of the equation are gaining traction. As we know, only three percent of a population is needed to sway popular opinion, so we have reasons to be optimistic.

And so, with Lord Tennyson I say, "Come, my friends, 'tis not too late to seek a newer world."

While seeking the newer world, always remember this—make it the wellspring, the inexhaustible fountainhead of your work: *We can halt and reverse ecological collapse.*

Dear Reader,

If you enjoyed this book, would you kindly write a short review? Reviews help others find this urgent message.

Thank you,

The Publisher

While seeking the newer world, always remember this—make it the wellspring, the inexhaustible fountainhead of your work: *We can halt and reverse ecological collapse.*